The Complete Guide to
FLOORING

Third Edition

Updated with New Products & Techniques

Creative Publishing
international

MINNEAPOLIS, MINNESOTA
www.creativepub.com

Creative Publishing international

Copyright © 2010
Creative Publishing international, Inc.
400 First Avenue North, Suite 300
Minneapolis, Minnesota 55401
1-800-328-0590
www.creativepub.com

Printed in China

10 9 8 7 6 5 4 3 2 1

Library of Congress Cataloging-in-Publication Data

The complete guide to flooring.
     p. cm.
  "Black & Decker."
  Includes index.
  Summary: "Features current favorites, repair & refinish, wood,
laminate, tile, carpet & more"--Provided by publisher.
  ISBN-13: 978-1-58923-521-2 (soft cover)
  ISBN-10: 1-58923-521-5 (soft cover)
  1. Flooring. I. Black & Decker Corporation (Towson, Md.) II. Title.

TH2521.C625 2010
690'.16--dc22

2010004486

President/CEO: Ken Fund

Home Improvement Group

Publisher: Bryan Trandem
Managing Editor: Tracy Stanley
Senior Editor: Mark Johanson

Creative Director: Michele Lanci-Altomare
Art Direction/Design: Brad Springer, Jon Simpson, James Kegley

Lead Photographer: Joel Schnell
Set Builder: James Parmeter
Production Managers: Linda Halls, Laura Hokkanen

Page Layout Artist: Danielle Smith
Shop Help: Charles Boldt
Edition Editor: Charles Peterson
Technical Editor: Betsy Matheson
Proofreader: Drew Siqveland

Cover photo © Photolibrary

The Complete Guide to Flooring
Created by: The Editors of Creative Publishing international, Inc., in cooperation with Black & Decker.
Black & Decker® is a trademark of The Black & Decker Corporation and is used under license.

NOTICE TO READERS

Contents

The Complete Guide to Flooring

Introduction 7

Planning Your New Floor 9

Planning Overview 10

Floor Anatomy 11

Floor Selection & Design 14

Inspiration 26

Project Preparation 47

Tools 48

Floor Covering Removal 50

Underlayment Removal 56

Subfloor Repair 58

Joist Repair 60

Preparing the Base 63

Underlayment 64

Basement Floors 72

Attic Floors 76

Underfloor Radiant Heat Systems 80

Contents (Cont.)

Installations **87**

Hardwood Floors 88

Bonded Bamboo Strip Flooring 102

Parquet Tiles 108

Floating Laminate Floors 112

Vinyl Plank Flooring 118

Linoleum Tile 122

Resilient Tile 126

Cork Tile 132

Recycled Rubber Tile 136

Ceramic, Stone & Glass Tile 140

Mosaic Tile 152

Combination Tile 156

Porcelain Snap-lock Tile 160

Interlocking Utility Tile 164

Bonded Rubber Roll Flooring 168

Seamed Rubber Roll Flooring 172

Resilient Sheet Vinyl 174

Carpet 184

Carpet Squares 208

Finishes & Surface Treatments 213

Floor Stains & Finishes. 214

Painting Wood Floors 218

Finishing Concrete Floors 222

Refinishing Hardwood Floors. 228

Repairs 235

Fixing Squeaky Floors 236

Replacing Trim Moldings 240

Repairing Hardwood 242

Replacing Laminate Planks 248

Repairing Resilient Flooring 252

Repairing Carpet 256

Repairing Tile 258

Resources 266

Photography Credits 266

Conversion Charts 267

Index 268

Introduction

Homeowners in search of just the right flooring have never before had more options. It's a pretty safe bet that no matter what your budget, DIY expertise, or décor preference, you'll find a flooring solution that perfectly suits your needs and tastes. In fact, you'll probably find multiple suitable flooring options from which to choose.

Time-tested hard floor surfacing, such as wood and tile, continue to be attractive and popular options for long-lasting floors with an enticing assortment of beautiful surfaces. Whether you prefer the warmth and glow of oak, or the show-stopping colors and veining of marble, these tried-and-true floors provide excellent solutions for just about any room or area in your house.

To go along with the traditional choices, technology has expanded flooring possibilities in recent years, most significantly in the forms of resilient flooring and laminate flooring. Resilient floors have a soft, giving surface, and long established options such as linoleum and vinyl are now complemented by a diversity of new offerings. Linoleum flooring is an older product that has much in common with resilient sheet flooring, but is made with natural products. In its original form it requires some experience and skill to install, but newer, DIY-friendly versions, often sold in strips or panels, are easier to install and still offer the pleasing characteristics of the original. Laminate flooring is a popular manufactured product that provides some cushion underfoot and an appearance that mimics other floor types, such as wood or slate.

These new types of flooring are complemented by new innovations in installation technology. You can choose from click together, glue-together, or stick-down floors as alternatives to more traditional and time-consuming methods.

Ultimately, the ideal floor covering for any room in your home is simply the one that has the right look and feel for the spot, while fitting into your budget. The only real limitation you face, given the amazing abundance of choices, is that you don't have more floors to cover in your house.

Planning Your New Floor

Like any successful remodeling project, replacing your floor covering requires detailed planning and attention to design. Flooring is not separate from the rest of the room; it should fit into the overall design to create a desired effect. A floor can create excitement and become a focal point or it can serve as a background for the rest of the room.

Through careful planning, you can choose flooring to be used successfully in multiple rooms, or select a pattern or design to repeat throughout the room or in adjacent rooms.

Keep in mind that your flooring design will last a long time, especially if you install ceramic tile or wood. In most cases, the only way to change the design of your floor is to install a new floor covering.

The information in this section will help you plan and design floors that meet your needs. After looking through the portfolio section for ideas of various floor coverings, you may also want to visit a flooring showroom to find the color, style, and pattern of the material you want to use. Then, following the directions in the remaining sections of this book, you can create a new look and feel for your living space.

In this chapter:

- Planning Overview
- Floor Anatomy
- Floor Selection & Design
- Inspiration

Planning Overview

A floor is one of the most visible parts of your decor, which is why appearance is a primary consideration when choosing floor coverings. Start your search by collecting ideas and inspiration from magazines and books, and visit retail flooring showrooms and home centers to get a sense of what your options are.

As important as appearance is, there are many other considerations that will go into your flooring decision. You'll no doubt put your budget near the top of the list, but you should think about how easy the floor will be to install, how comfortable it is underfoot, its longevity and durability, its resistance to moisture, and how easy it is to clean. You'll also need to assess the demands of the space, including moisture, heavy traffic, and other conditions.

When estimating materials for your project, always add 10 to 15 percent to the total square footage to allow for waste in installation (some carpet installations may require even more). And always save extra flooring materials just in case you ever need to make a repair.

Measure the area of the project room to calculate the quantity of materials you'll need. Measure the full width and length of the space to determine the overall square footage, then subtract the areas that will not be covered, such as stairways, cabinets, and other permanent fixtures.

Checklist for Planning a Flooring Project ▸

Use this checklist to organize your activities as you start your flooring project.

- Measure the project area carefully. Be sure to include all nooks and closets, as well as areas under all movable appliances. Calculate the total square footage of the project area.
- Use your measurements to create a floor plan on graph paper.
- Sketch pattern options on tracing paper laid over the floor plan to help you visualize what the flooring will look like after you install it.
- Identify areas where the type of floor covering will change, and choose the best threshold material to use for the transition.
- Estimate the amount of preparation material needed, including underlayment sheets and floor leveler.
- Estimate the amount of installation material needed, including the floor covering and other supplies, such as adhesive, grout, thresholds, tackless strips, and screws. Add 10 to 15% to your total square footage to allow for waste caused by trimming. For some carpet installations you will need to add even more. *Tip: For help in estimating, go to a building supply center and read the labels on materials and adhesives to determine coverage.*

- Make a list of the tools needed for the job. Locate sources for the tools you will need to buy or rent.
- Estimate the total cost of the project, including all preparation materials, flooring, installation materials, and tools. For expensive materials, shop around to get the best prices.
- Check with building supply centers or flooring retail stores for delivery costs. A delivery service is often worth the additional charge.
- Determine how much demolition you will need to do, and plan for debris removal through your regular garbage collector or a disposal company.
- Plan for the temporary displacement of furnishings and removable appliances to minimize disruption of your daily routine.

Floor Anatomy

A typical wood-frame floor consists of layers that work together to provide the required structural support and desired appearance. These parts include:

1. Joists. At the bottom of the floor are the joists, 2×10 or larger framing members that support the weight of the floor. Joists are typically spaced 16 inches apart on center.
2. Subfloor. The subfloor is nailed to the joists. Most subfloors installed in the 1970s or later are made of ¾-inch tongue-and-groove plywood; in older houses, the subfloor often consists of one-inch-thick wood planks nailed diagonally across the floor joists.
3. Underlayment. On top of the subfloor, most builders place a ½-inch plywood underlayment. Some flooring materials, especially ceramic tile, require cementboard for stability.
4. Adhesive. For many types of floor coverings, adhesive or mortar is spread on the underlayment before the floor covering is installed. Carpet rolls generally require tackless strips and cushioned padding.
5. Floorcovering. Other materials, such as snap-fit laminate planks or carpet squares, can be installed directly on the underlayment with little or no adhesive.

Asbestos & Flooring ▸

Resilient flooring manufactured before 1980 may contain asbestos, which can cause severe lung problems if inhaled. The easiest method for dealing with asbestos-containing flooring is to cover it with a new floorcovering. If the asbestos flooring must be removed, consult an asbestos-abatement professional or ask a local building inspector to explain the asbestos handling and disposal regulations in your area.

Cutaway of a Typical Floor

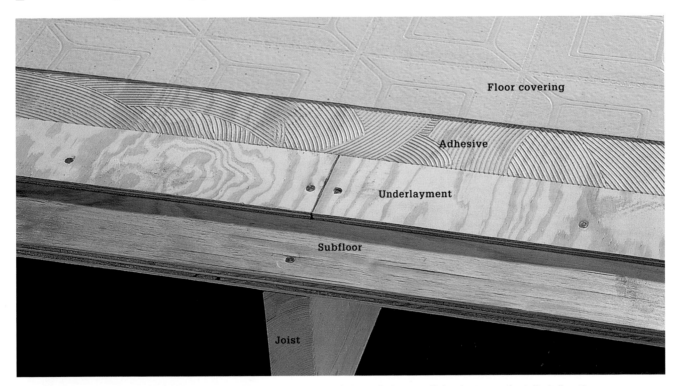

Not all floor covering materials require adhesive; some materials, such as snap-fit laminate, are installed directly on the underlayment.

RESILIENT FLOORING

Option 1: Your existing resilient floor can serve as the foundation for most new floor coverings, including resilient flooring, hardwood, and carpet, but only if the existing surface is relatively smooth and sound. Inspect the existing flooring for loose seams, tears, chips, air bubbles, and other areas where the bond has failed. If these loose spots constitute less than 30% of the total area, you can remove the flooring at these spots and fill the voids with floor-leveling compound. Then, apply embossing leveler to the entire floor and let it dry before laying new flooring.

Option 2: If the original resilient flooring is suspect, you can install new underlayment over the old surface after repairing obviously loose areas.

Option 3: If you're installing ceramic tile, or if the existing surface is in very poor condition, the old resilient flooring should be removed entirely before you install new flooring. If the old flooring was glued down with full-bond adhesive, it's usually easiest to remove both the flooring and underlayment at the same time. If the old underlayment is removed, you must install new underlayment before laying the new flooring.

CERAMIC TILE

Option 1: If the existing ceramic tile surface is relatively solid, new flooring can usually be laid directly over the tile. Inspect tiles and joints for cracks and loose pieces. Remove loose material and fill these areas with a floor-leveling compound. If you're installing resilient flooring, apply an embossing leveler product over the ceramic tile before laying the new flooring. If you're laying new ceramic tile over the old surface, use an epoxy-based thin-set mortar for better adhesion.

Option 2: If more than 10% of the tiles are loose, remove all of the old flooring before installing the new surface. If the tiles don't easily separate from the underlayment, it's best to remove the tile and the underlayment at the same time, then install new underlayment.

HARDWOOD FLOORING

Option 1: If you're installing carpet, you can usually lay it directly over an existing hardwood floor, provided it's a nailed or glued-down surface. Inspect the flooring and secure any loose areas to the subfloor with spiral-shanked

flooring nails, then remove any rotted wood and fill the voids with floor-leveling compound before installing the carpet.

Option 2: If you're installing resilient flooring or ceramic tile over nailed hardwood planks or glued-down wood flooring, attach new underlayment over the existing hardwood before installing the new flooring.

Option 3: If the existing floor is a "floating" wood or laminate surface with a foam-pad underlayment, remove it completely before laying any type of new flooring.

UNDERLAYMENT & SUBFLOOR

Underlayment must be smooth, solid, and level to ensure a long-lasting flooring installation. If the existing underlayment does not meet these standards, remove it and install new underlayment before you lay new flooring.

Before installing new underlayment, inspect the subfloor for chips, open knots, dips, and loose boards. Screw down loose areas, and fill cracks and dips with floor-leveling compound. Remove and replace any water-damaged areas.

CARPET

Without exception, carpet must be removed before you install any new flooring. For traditional carpet, simply cut the carpet into pieces, then remove the padding and the tackless strips. Remove glued-down cushion-back carpet with a floor scraper, using the same techniques as for removing full-bond resilient sheet flooring (see page 53).

Establish a logical work sequence. Many flooring projects are done as part of a more comprehensive remodeling project. In this case, the flooring should be installed after the walls and ceiling are finished, but before the fixtures are installed. Protect new flooring with heavy paper or tarps when completing your remodeling project.

Evaluating Floors

When installing new flooring over old, measure vertical spaces to make sure enclosed or under-counter appliances will fit once the new underlayment and flooring are installed. Use samples of the new underlayment and floor covering as spacers when measuring.

High thresholds often indicate that several layers of flooring have already been installed on top of one another. If you have several layers, it's best to remove them before installing the new floor covering.

Buckling in solid hardwood floors indicates that the boards have loosened from the subfloor. Do not remove hardwood floors. Instead, refasten loose boards by drilling pilot holes and inserting flooring nails or screws. New carpet can be installed right over a well-fastened hardwood floor. New ceramic tile or resilient flooring should be installed over underlayment placed on the hardwood flooring.

Loose tiles may indicate widespread failure of the adhesive. Use a wallboard knife to test tiles. If tiles can be pried up easily in many different areas of the room, plan to remove all of the flooring.

Air bubbles trapped under resilient sheet flooring indicate that the adhesive has failed. The old flooring must be removed before the new covering can be installed.

Cracks in grout joints around ceramic tile are a sign that movement of the floor covering has caused deterioration of the adhesive layer. If more than 10% of the tiles are loose, remove the old flooring. Evaluate the condition of the underlayment (see opposite page) to determine if it also must be removed.

Floor Selection & Design

Wood

Solid wood flooring is a favorite with homeowners for good reason. The exceptional variety of species means that you can find a look to match just about any decor. The material itself is durable, natural, and extremely long-lasting. Wood floors are comfortable underfoot, relatively easy to install, and competitive in price with stone or ceramic tile. Plus, you can choose from a wealth of wood finish colors and patinas for a customized appearance.

The species of wood you choose has a dramatic influence on the floor's final appearance. The most common parquet species is oak, which has a tight grain with little variation in pattern and coloring. Oak is a good option in homes with bold decorative elements—such as vibrant fixtures or colorful furniture—or in rooms that merit a nice floor underfoot to complement a simple interior. Some wood species, such as cherry and exotic woods, feature strong variations in grain pattern, shading, and hue from board to board. These are best used in floors that are meant to stand out on their own, serving as a dynamic, attention-getting element of the decor.

When selecting wood flooring, consider the dimensions of the floorboards. Traditional hardwood flooring is sold in narrow strips that are approximately 2¼ inches wide. Solid hardwood often comes in random lengths, but hardwood-veneer flooring is usually sold in standard lengths of three, four, or six feet. Planks range from 3½ to more than 12 inches in width and create a distinctive, informal look in a living room or any open-floor-plan area. Wide plank flooring usually is made of lumber from the pine family. Parquet is a formal floorcovering created by edge-gluing solid strips or squares of wood into tile shapes and then laying them in a pattern, such as herringbone. Parquet floors are most often used in formal areas like entry foyers, or throughout period-style homes featuring other formal decorative elements. Parquet is available in standard ¾-inch thickness and in a "thin profile" ⁵⁄₁₆-inch-thick product suitable for installing over a concrete slab.

The type of wood finish you use has a major impact on the floor's appearance. If the wood is naturally interesting, you'll probably want to finish it with a clear, protective topcoat, such as polyurethane floor varnish. Natural wood flooring can be stained in shades from blonde to nearly black, colored with tints, ebonized for a truly black floor, or even painted for a truly individual look. It is worth noting that professional floor finishers seldom color the wood because scratches that penetrate the color layer are highly visible. Most solid wood flooring types are also available prefinished.

Hardwood strip flooring (oak)

Natural hardwoods create an environment of warmth and comfort. From the floor to window sashes and fireplace trim, wood materials combine practicality and luxury.

Parquet floor tiles

Exotic Options ▶

Availability of wood species varies regionally, but most common North American hardwoods are used in the manufacture of flooring. Stock options typically are limited to oak and maple, with cherry, ash, mahogany, walnut, and several other species easily obtained through special order. These North American woods give you plenty of choices for your floor, but even more stunning options are available if you're willing to spend a bit more. Imported "exotic" species bring with them distinctive and stunning patterns and colors. A sampling includes:

Ipé (Brazil). The Brazilian walnut tree yields boards with grain patterns ranging from regular to very irregular, and an attractive reddish-brown color.

Wenge (Africa). A naturally deep, dark brown—almost black—wood, wenge has long been used for fine wood furnishings. The alluring grain structure appears prominently, and the wood is at its most showy cut in wider planks.

Patagonian Rosewood (Chile). A distinctive option, Rosewood has dark tan colors that lighten over time, and features bold striping throughout the grain that adds an interesting undertone to the natural luster of the wood.

Cumaru (Brazil). A coarse, wavy grain and a reddish tan color that fades over time into an unusual maroon, make this wood an interesting choice. Also called Brazilian Teak.

Tigerwood (Latin America). A lighter wood, Tigerwood has a unique, extremely irregular, and interlocking grain structure from which it gets its name. The color generally varies from deep golden brown to almost blond. Tigerwood is best placed in an open, well-lit space, with large uncovered areas showing off the eye-catching grain.

ECO-FRIENDLY WOOD FLOORING

Wood is one of the most environmentally sound flooring options. It's a renewable resource, it doesn't give off harmful chemicals, and it can be recycled or composted at the end of its life. Harvesting raw lumber has become more eco-friendly as modern forest management practices have been put into effect. As a consumer, you can do your part to ensure that your wood floor is helping conserve precious resources by looking for the Forest Stewardship Council (FSC) label on the flooring. The label indicates that the wood comes from forests that are certified and well-managed according to the rules of the Council.

Another way to help preserve forests is to choose reclaimed flooring. Recycled floors are made of boards rescued from buildings that were demolished; reclaimed wood flooring is salvaged from the timbers of old structures, such as warehouses or barns, or from discarded wood. As a bonus, reclaimed and recycled woods often offer extremely unique surface appearances.

Bamboo (although technically a grass, not a wood) is another eco-friendly alternative. Manufactured in strips and installed the same way as solid wood floors, bamboo makes for a durable and interesting floor. It is a fast-growing plant and the harvesting process has minimal environmental impact, so bamboo floors are considered one of the "greenest" floors you can choose.

FSC-Certified Wood ▶

The Forest Stewardship Council (FSC) is an international nonprofit group that certifies forests and wood products based on established standards of responsible forest management. Products bearing the FSC stamp have been monitored by third-party officials from the raw material stage in the forest through processing, manufacturing, and distribution as part of their "chain of custody" standards. FSC certification is the best way to ensure that wood products and materials come from sustainable, renewable sources, just like all wood should. For more information, visit www.fsc.org.

Reclaimed flooring is salvaged from old buildings. In some cases, it is remilled and looks brand new; sometimes it is installed essentially as it was found.

Bamboo flooring is formed by pressing strands of bamboo fiber together with binders. Bamboo is a highly renewable resource.

ENGINEERED WOOD FLOORING

On the quality scale, engineered wood flooring lies somewhere between solid hardwood flooring and all-synthetic laminate flooring. Engineered flooring strips are composed of a thin veneer top layer over two layers of plywood that are positioned perpendicular to one another. This construction gives the engineered wood floor a great deal of strength, and a comparable surface texture and feel to hardwood flooring. Because the surface is actual wood, engineered wood floors are generally made from the same species as solid hardwood floors. But engineered floors are usually sold prefinished and are often installed with snap-together joints similar to laminate floors. Engineered floors are also easier on a budget than solid wood. The downside to engineered flooring with a real-wood wear layer is that in most cases they can only be sanded and refinished once.

LAMINATE FLOORING

Laminate flooring has taken over a large share of the DIY flooring market in recent years because it is easy to install and relatively inexpensive. Sold in strips or small panels that look like strips, it is constructed of a base layer of wood product to which is bonded a photographic pattern layer that replicates wood (or sometimes nonwood) floor coverings. It is sold prefinished with a clear, protective wear-layer of highly durable aluminum oxide.

Although some laminate flooring is installed by edge-gluing, nearly all product sold today is put down as a floating floor with click-together joints that have a positive locking action, requiring no fasteners or adhesives (although in many cases, a perimeter bond is recommended). Grain patterns and coloring are uniform and consistent across the strips (or, in some cases, tiles), making a completed laminate floor unchallenging for the eye.

Many types of laminates are water resistant, making them good alternatives to solid wood floors in moisture-prone areas, such as below-grade basements and bathrooms. Check the manufacturer's warranty for moisture-resistance information for the flooring you're considering.

Real-wood veneer flooring has a layer of durable wood veneer that looks and wears like solid wood.

Laminate flooring has taken over a huge chunk of the DIY market because it is inexpensive and easy to install.

Resilient Flooring

As the name implies, resilient flooring has a soft, yielding surface that "bounces back" and is warm and comfortable underfoot. It is also moisture-resistant and provides a bit of cushion in the event of the occasional dropped glass (which is why resilient flooring is a favorite for kitchens and baths). The three basic types of resilient flooring are vinyl, linoleum, and laminate. Vinyl and linoleum are available in tile and sheet form, while laminates are offered as strips and tiles.

Vinyl is a durable synthetic with a surface layer printed using a photographic method known as "rotogravure." This process allows for the reproduction of an almost unlimited variety of colors, patterns, and designs, including realistic depictions of natural materials such as wood or stone. Vinyl flooring can also be molded to create different surface textures,

from perfectly smooth to pebbly. Vinyl sheet flooring is sold in six- and 12-foot-wide rolls that are backed with either PVC, felt, or fiberglass. The backing affects the installation process that must be used: edge gluing (known as the *perimeter-bond* method) is used with PVC backing, while felt-backed vinyl is fully glued down (the *full-spread* method). Fiberglass-backed vinyl is installed without glue. Vinyl tiles come with a self-adhesive backing (often called "sticky-backs") or without adhesive.

Vinyl is an attractive, economical floor choice for high-use rooms such as basement playrooms, kitchens, bathrooms, and laundry rooms. If you're using vinyl in a high-traffic area such as a busy kitchen or kids' bathroom, use a thick version (65 mils or thicker) with an enhanced urethane topcoat for additional

Resilient sheet vinyl floors have a moisture-resistant surface and are installed as a single sheet (sometimes with glued seams).

Resilient tile floors also have a moisture-resistant surface. The tiles are set into a thin bed of adhesive.

protection. This type is normally laid flat with only perimeter bonding.

Linoleum was once a modern, popular floor covering—but that was over 100 years ago. Although it's still available in sheet form, sheet linoleum is a temperamental material that usually requires professional installation because of its tendency to shrink and expand. Although a modern version of linoleum is available in sheets, the best way for a DIYer to add the natural look and soft feel of real linoleum is with linoleum-topped tiles that are installed as a floating floor system (*Marmoleum* is one leading brand—see Resources, page 266).

Both linoleum and marmoleum are produced with saturated colors in many shades, from sedate neutrals to bold, blazing hues. The appearance is enhanced with designs that range from mottled to speckled to irregular montages of graphic shapes and figures.

Aside from the visual appeal, linoleum products are noteworthy for their environmentally friendly nature. They are made with all-natural ingredients, including linseed oil, wood flour, resins, ground natural pigments, and other organic additives. The flooring doesn't cause interior air quality to degrade because it does not off-gas volatile organic compounds as many other flooring types and flooring finishes do. Linoleum is also hypoallergenic and even has antibacterial properties. Linoleum is biodegradable, so when the time comes to replace it—not a common occurrence for flooring that can easily last decades— the material can be discarded with the knowledge that it will quickly and safely break down. The longevity of this material merits a cautious approach to choosing from among the multitude of colors and fanciful patterns available; you'll likely be living with the floor for a long time, so avoid trendy styles.

Linoleum is a natural floor covering that has been around for more than a century.

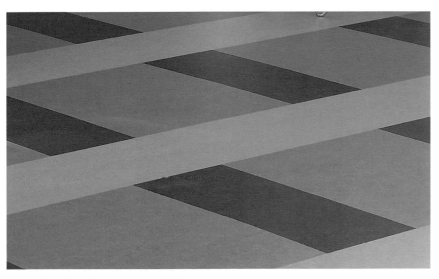

Linoleum tiles offer many of the benefits of linoleum, but in a package that's more DIY friendly.

Ceramic & Stone Tiles

Hard tile floors made from ceramic or stone are well-suited for kitchens and bathrooms where the material—whether kiln-fired clay or quarried stone—naturally resists moisture and stands up to the high-traffic demands of those rooms. But ceramic and stone tiles are seeing increased usage elsewhere in the house; particularly in foyers, entryways, and in family rooms where a stain-resistant floorcovering that's easy to clean is desirable. Choose hard tiles carefully, because most types can last for decades or longer with proper care and maintenance.

Ceramic tiles remain the most common type of hard flooring because they are generally less expensive than stone, and the potential designs are virtually unlimited. Ceramic tiles are also easy to clean and fairly durable. They can be left natural as a specific style indicator, as is the case with terra cotta, or they can be custom-painted with intricate designs. The designs may be contained within a single tile, or part of a larger design element such as a border, with a pattern that flows from tile to tile. The tiles can also be sealed with finishes ranging from high-gloss to matte. However, ceramic tiles tend to be brittle and are easily cracked if, say, a heavy appliance is accidentally dropped on one. They are also cold floors underfoot and don't offer the surface variations that stone floors do. Porcelain tile is a type of ceramic tile that is very popular for floors, both interior and exterior. It is harder and more durable than regular ceramic tiles, but it also is much more time consuming to cut.

Stone tiles present an incredible diversity of looks and textures. Expense will certainly drive your choice to some degree, but keep in mind the remarkable longevity of the material makes it more affordable in the long run.

Considered the king of tiles, marble screams luxury. Intricate veining and colors that run the gamut, from subtle and elegant whites and beiges to dramatic fiery reds and jade greens, ensure that marble floors will always be an attention-getter. But that showy nature is why marble is usually reserved for formal rooms and well-appointed decor that can hold up the sumptuous elegance of the stone. Lavish master baths, wide-open foyers with sweeping staircases, and other dramatic, light-filled spaces are ideal candidates for a marble floor. Its beauty isn't cheap; marble is one of the most expensive tile types, and the more unique the coloration and veining, the more expensive the marble. It also requires regular maintenance, and is susceptible to staining from various liquids, including water, juices, and shampoos.

The most popular stone floor tile, granite is sold in an array of interesting colors, from subdued grays, to purples, deep greens, and even black. The stone features coarse-to-fine speckling and striking mottled patterns, and the finish can be an elegant high gloss or a non-slip matte. In either case, granite is durable and stain resistant, and scratches can be buffed out of the surface.

Limestone and sandstone are similar types of stones that provide interesting alternatives to marble

Ceramic tile is a popular floorcovering with DIYers because it is durable, relatively easy to install and the types at the lower end of the price scale are quite affordable.

Ceramic floor tiles are typically between ³⁄₁₆" and ½" in thickness. Common sizes include squares ranging from 8 × 8" up to 13 × 13" and bigger, as well as 12 × 12" mosaic sheets.

Cut stone tiles combine the natural beauty of stone with the ease of installation and uniform sizes of ceramic tile.

Granite tiles can be used on floors or countertops. When installed, the tiny gaps between tiles are filled with matching filler or grout so the surface looks homogenous.

Patio and walkway stone, such as flagstone or cut slate, are lending their natural beauty and drama to interior settings at a rapidly growing pace.

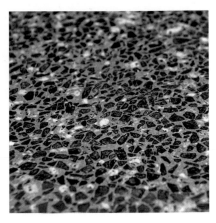

Terrazzo is a manmade, hard tile that possesses the overall look and feel of elegant marble, but at a lower price and in standard sizes.

or granite. More susceptible to wear because they are softer, both provide a warm feel and sophisticated appearance that is well suited even to living rooms or dining rooms. Limestone and sandstone are both porous and should be sealed to prevent moisture and dirt infiltration, and both are available in restrained hues limited to tans, beiges, and grays.

Once limited to use as outdoor flooring, slate tiles are increasingly finding a place in kitchens, dining rooms, and informal entry halls. No wonder, given the dramatic appearance of this hard and dense stone. You'll find amazing color and patterns among these tiles, from saturated jet black to appealingly dusty reds, blues, and greens. All are arrestingly beautiful, resistant to moisture and stains, and good at hiding dirt.

A cousin to limestone and sandstone, travertine features extremely understated patterns and colors (mostly beige) that make it complementary to most decors. It can be square cut, sealed, and polished to resemble marble, or left rough and pitted for a more "country villa" look. In any case, it must be carefully treated to produce a cleanable, non-porous surface.

Terrazzo is a manmade flooring material created by blending marble chips with cement or epoxy. The process allows manufacturers to control the end result, so terrazzo boasts an impressive, nearly limitless variety of colors and patterns. The appearance can also be varied by changing the size of fragments used. Patterns range from fine-grained to coarse, with smoothly blended monotones or a mixture of colors.

Terrazzo is most often blended and laid as a complete floor on site, but the flooring is now available in slabs and tiles. However, even these smaller versions are best installed by an experienced flooring professional.

Glass Tiles

Glass floor tiles bring an incomparable spark to the right space. Glass tile colors are unusually vibrant and luminous with a lit-from-within nature. Because the glass is carefully annealed (a process that hardens it), glass tiles are far more durable than they might appear to be. Available in a vast selection of shining, semi-translucent colors and surface finishes, from frosted to etched, these tiles are appropriate for a surprisingly wide range of contemporary and modern decors.

Glass tiles have a translucent quality that makes them practically glow in a floor setting. Most are sold and installed in mosaic sheets.

Carpet

No flooring can rival carpet for sheer comfort underfoot. The combination of soft fibers and cushioned padding is what makes carpet a favorite throughout the house, especially in casual areas like bedrooms, where walking barefoot is the norm. How luxurious the carpet feels underfoot, and the overall quality and durability of the material, depends on the type of fiber used and the "pile," or fiber profile, of the carpet. The type and thickness of the carpet pad also bear directly on the feel underfoot.

The most common types of carpet fibers are synthetics, including nylon, acrylic, polyester, and polypropylene (also known as olefin). Acrylic is rarely used in today's wall-to-wall carpet application because its feel underfoot and its resistance to dirt and wear can't match the other fibers. Nylon is the most popular carpet fiber because of its durability, natural resistance to wear and stains, and soft feel. Nylon carpeting also holds up well over time.

Polyester is also a popular fiber because of its ability to hold brilliant colors. It is stain- and fade-resistant, but is more susceptible to crushing than nylon, making it a poor candidate for high-traffic rooms. Some forms of polyester carpets are made from recycled plastic bottles and all polyester is non-allergenic, making this fiber the greenest of the synthetics.

Polypropylene fibers are the toughest of the lot. They are extremely resistant to stains, as well as moisture, mildew, and shedding. The feel is almost as good as nylon, explaining why this type of fiber has quickly become nylon's chief competitor.

Wool is a naturally luxurious and long-lasting carpet fiber option, and is by far the softest and most elegant fiber. Lower quality wool is not as stain- or soil-resistant as synthetics, however, and high grade wool is expensive. Many carpeting manufacturers blend wool fibers with synthetics to leverage the benefits of each type.

Carpet is comfortable underfoot and can be installed over inexpensive subfloor and underlayment, making it potentially one of the most affordable floor systems.

Synthetic carpet fibers are economical and generally resist staining well. High quality synthetics have a rich, luxurious feel, while lower quality versions have an inescapable plastic quality.

Wool and wool-blend carpeting has declined in popularity due to its higher cost, but if you can afford it, you can be confident you'll love the material.

Carpet Pile ▸

Of course fibers are only half the story when it comes to evaluating carpet. The other half is the pile. Carpet is made by looping yarn through a backing. The loops can be cut, left intact, or a combination of both can be used to create textures. Density is another factor in the quality of the carpet. The more fibers packed into a given area, the greater the resistance to dirt and wear and tear.

Loop-pile carpet has a sculpted appearance. Loops can be arranged randomly or they can make a distinct repeating pattern. Loop pile is a good choice for high-traffic areas because the loops resist crushing and won't show footprints or vacuum marks.

Velvet-cut pile carpet is the densest of any carpet type and is cut so that the color remains uniform when the pile is brushed in any direction. Velvets are well suited to formal living spaces.

Saxony-cut pile (also known as plush) is specifically constructed to resist matting and crushing better than velvet cut-pile. The pile is trimmed at a bevel, giving it a speckled appearance.

When choosing roll carpet, always check the label, which will tell you the fiber type and number of twists; pile density; available widths of the roll (usually 12 or 15 feet); stain, soil, and other treatments; and the length of the warranty.

Cushion-backed

Loop-pile

Velvet-cut pile

Saxony-cut pile

Carpet tiles have become increasingly popular over the past decade. These are offered with the same pile options as roll carpeting, but in a cushioned-backed square tile format that is not only easy to lay, it also aids design. Because you buy the carpet tiles by the box, you can easily mix and match colors and patterns or, in the case of some manufacturers, photographic representations.

Tiles are much easier to install or remove than other types of carpeting. They are stuck to a level, clean subfloor surface with small adhesive patches supplied by the manufacturer. Some higher-end carpet tile has a thick backing that is designed to lay flat and stay put without any adhesives.

Installing carpet tiles (also called carpet squares) is about as easy as a flooring project can be. Many homeowners are attracted to the reversibility of carpet tiles—if you don't like them, you can rearrange them easily.

Design

No matter what type of floor you install, choose your colors, patterns, and textures carefully. You may have to live with your choices for years—or even decades. Flooring is one of the most visible elements of interior design, which makes it one of the most important.

Flooring can serve as a bold, eye-catching design statement, or an understated background. Whatever approach you take, always consider the design of the adjoining rooms when choosing flooring. Because floors flow from one room to the next, floor coverings offer a convenient medium for creating continuity throughout your home. This does not mean you should use the same floor covering in every room. Simply repeating a color, pattern, or texture can be enough to provide continuity.

The examples on these pages help illustrate how your choice of color, pattern, and texture can affect the look and feel of a room.

Always carefully consider how your floor covering choice will affect the decor of the rest of the room; compare color swatches and samples to make sure your final choice is the best one.

Create design continuity by using the same flooring in adjacent rooms. Borders can help define separate spaces, as seen here in the dining area.

Color of flooring influences the visual impact of a room. Bold, bright colors draw attention, while muted colors create a neutral background that doesn't compete for attention. Colors also affect the perceived size of a room. Dark colors are formal in tone, but can make a room look smaller. Light colors are more contemporary, and can make the room seem larger.

Pattern of flooring affects the feeling and tone of a room. In general, subtle patterns lend a more relaxed feel to a room and can make it appear larger. Bold, recurring patterns create excitement and focal points for a room. Choose your flooring pattern carefully to ensure it doesn't clash with other patterns in the room.

Texture of flooring contributes to the style of a room. More rugged surfaces, such as slate or loop-pile carpet, give a room a warm, earthy tone. Smooth and glossy surfaces, such as polished marble tile or hardwood flooring, impart an airy sense of elegance.

Inspiration

The perfect floor is an integral component of any interior design. A well-chosen floor covering will interact with other design elements in the room. The flooring should also be practical and fit the needs of each room. For example, in a kitchen where spills are common, sheet vinyl or ceramic tile is a more practical choice than expensive, deep-pile wool carpet. In a formal dining room, wood parquet is more fitting than resilient tile.

The photos in this section highlight a wide range of flooring types and materials for any room in the home. The following pages are sure to give you new ideas for creative ways to meet your flooring needs.

Natural hardwoods create an environment of warmth and comfort. From the floor to window sashes and fireplace trim, wood materials combine practicality and luxury.

The medallion in this foyer is sure to catch the eyes of all those who enter this home because of its color and pattern. By incorporating a medallion that is the same material as the surrounding floor and steps, it stands as a subtle and sophisticated detail.

A floor can be the leading design feature in a room from which all other elements in the room follow. In this room, the stone tile floor is the focal point. Smaller tiles around the fireplace echo the pattern set down on the floor surface below.

The richness and depth of color, along with the wide wood grain, give this floor covering all the appeal of an exotic hardwood. It is actually linoleum, however, which is made principally from linseed oil, rosin, limestone and natural pigments.

Sometimes, the beauty of simplicity provides the most satisfying results. The tiles that provide a design base for this entryway will last for years, even decades. Thanks to their neutral color and pattern, they can complement many styles as the homeowners decide to change other elements in the room.

Hardwood strips and planks are the most common wood floor coverings. Hardwood doesn't compete with other decor elements in a room, yet it makes a definitive statement. This floor uses two different woods to create an appealing border around the kitchen island.

This resilient floor combines several subdued colors for a contemporary look. Because the tones are slightly darker than the walls and furniture, the floor grounds the room and serves as a base focal point.

Square and rectangular ceramic tiles can be combined for a sleek, sophisticated look. Laid on a diagonal, the floor tiles widen this long, narrow bathroom.

Wall-to-wall carpet is versatile and easily adopts the style and feel of the other room elements. The carpet in this family room takes on a sleek yet comfortable look. By choosing a color slightly lighter than the furniture, it acts as a subtle background for the homeowners' collections. The monochromatic theme of all elements enhances the spaciousness of the otherwise small room.

Gentle variations in color—such as wood products or laminates with wood-grain prints—soften the design of a room and create an overall warm tone. Whether you call it blonde or honey or natural, this floor deserves one description: beautiful.

Exclamations of color separated by bold black borders make up a dramatic resilient floor in this kitchen. The visual dividing lines do not correspond exactly with the room transitions, helping bring the spaces together. Look beyond the edges of a room to see more design opportunities.

Iridescent glass tiles, made from recycled material, appear at first glance to be two shades of blue. A closer look reveals that they reflect countless hues, depending on how the light strikes them. This arrangement works best in small rooms, where the scale of the tiles matches the space.

More than two colors alternating in an irregular pattern give this room a casual feel. The classic checkerboard design is muted to create a light and airy space. This attractive, simple design can be made with any material that is sold in squares.

A single color washed over the walls, sinks, and floor generates a cool, smooth, spa-like atmosphere. The sea blue in this room evokes the calm serenity of water. A soft brown rug provides a sandy beach for the eyes and feet.

Textured concrete floors can be both durable and beautiful. To create a textured surface, you can use stamping forms while the concrete is still wet. To add color as well, apply powdered dyes. This creates the look of stone, ceramic, or even marble. These treatments use a humble material to create a showpiece.

Carpet with just a little detail demands attention. Even though the surface is soft and relatively smooth, that small amount of texture enhances the visual interest of the carpet. In this room it also provides a gentle contrast to the plush bedding and sheer window coverings.

Mixed materials can have an interesting design effect, especially in transition areas such as this step down foyer. The contrast between the wood step and the geometric floor tiles also has an important safety feature, helping to draw attention to a step that would blend in visually (and somewhat invisibly) if it were tiled also.

A smooth tile floor like this has variations in color and rough-cut edges that give it character. The mottled rust and verdigris are reminiscent of aging bronze sculptures, while the grout lines look like the work of ancient master masons. In real life, however, you could install this floor yourself—today.

A checkerboard inside a checkerboard creates contrast in color, size, and shape. The effect draws your eye across the surface, while subdued brown tones provide an understated foundation for the surprise of bold red walls.

Natural hardwood flooring can vary significantly in color and grain from floorboard to floorboard. Although you can spend time up front trying to group your floorboards for more evenness of overall tone, the contrasting tones also make a nice design statement.

Wood parquet tiles can be combined into interesting patterns. Pay attention to grain direction as well as color when designing your parquet tile layout.

Bamboo strip flooring has high visual impact and, because it is derived from an easily renewable resource, it is considered one of the greener floor covering options. Since becoming a very popular option, bamboo has also come down in price relative to other floor coverings.

Regular and random at the same time, this floor makes a compromise by marrying solid and mottled blocks. Every row has the same width, but individual tiles within each row are not as structured. The result is a design that both follows a rhythm and breaks it.

A smooth blue floor is just about the coolest foundation possible for a bedroom. While leaving the rest of the white room airy and light, the checkerboard and solid blue field create a sense of quiet calm.

The warm tans and cool whites of this bathroom balance cleanliness and comfort. Despite using only right angles on the fixtures and walls, this sparsely decorated room maintains an elegant, informal appearance.

Limestone and glass establish a calm yet sophisticated atmosphere in this bathroom. Subtle variations in tile color provide visual interest; colored grout keeps the color family together.

A deep, rich stain on this hardwood floor gives the room a solid color foundation for the warm autumn colors on the walls and ceiling. Incandescent lights enhance the warm glow in the room.

Mixed materials can bring the best of both sound-reflecting and sound-absorbing qualities. In this example, a highly reflective hardwood surface becomes hushed by a small area rug. The hardwood's beauty remains visible, and the area rug complements the décor.

Glass mosaic tile brings bright, cheerful color and plenty of bouncing light into any room. It is especially popular in bathrooms. It is usually installed over a white subbase using white thinset mortar and white grout.

Marble tile is the pinnacle of elegance in a bathroom or foyer where hard, easily cleaned surfaces are preferred. The tiles themselves are butted much closer together than ceramic floor tiles, keeping grout hidden.

Concrete floors are now being welcomed into rooms beyond their traditional use in basements and garages. A variety of surface treatments can transform this utilitarian material into a fashionable floor. A few characteristics of concrete won't change, though: It's still hard, and it reflects sound. Offset these drawbacks with soft furniture and window coverings.

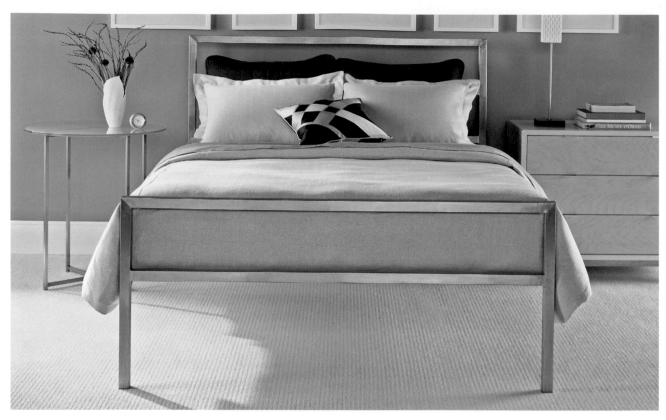

A luxurious carpet is a practical indulgence when the only shoes in the room are your bedroom slippers. Of course, you will want it to be durable, even if you treat it gently. Wool fibers are among the most long-wearing versions available, and Berber loops are especially comfortable on bare feet.

Ceramic tile holds up well under heavy use. But it can be tiring to stand on for long periods, and may feel cold underfoot. New layered products, combining ceramic and resilient materials, give you the look and feel of ceramic tile, with the warmth and easy installation of vinyl tile.

Quarry tile has been a favorite of commercial kitchens for decades. It stands up to heavy use day and night, and is easy to clean. It also has a naturally warm appearance that gives any kitchen a soft glow. Other popular places for quarry tile are bathrooms and spas.

Combining mosaic tile in a variety of colors and sizes produces elegant designs. Elaborate patterns can be deceptively easy to create with tile mounted to mesh backings. Even pre-arranged borders are widely available. Mosaic tile of any material is generally quite slip-resistant because of the many grout lines.

Wide plank bamboo flooring has a soft, contemporary appearance that blends nicely with modern wood furniture. It can be installed as a glue-down, or it can be nailed or stapled.

Click-together linoleum tiles have a soft, muted patina even when newly installed. They are a perfect choice for creating interesting patterns and blending colors. Tiles may be rectangular or square.

Leather may be the most fragile of all flooring materials. It's luxurious, but vulnerable to abrasion, tears, cuts, and damage from any sharp or rough object. The tile floor shown here has a faux leather appearance, but maintains the durability of ceramic tile.

Ceramic tile stair treads and risers create a durable, attractive surface. The hardwood nosing stands up better to the type of foot traffic stair nosing is subjected to, and it also makes a pleasing visual contrast.

This luxury vinyl tile offers the rugged beauty of cut stone, but with easy care. Its solid vinyl construction is more durable than traditional composition tile, and its top wear layer resists abrasion. Its greatest advantage over stone and ceramic tile is that vinyl never needs mortar or grout.

Bamboo floors have become very popular in the past few years. It's a grass, not a wood, so it grows quickly and is therefore more sustainable than wood. And the process of turning bamboo into flooring is ecologically friendly. Most important, it has the best qualities of hardwood with greater durability, value, and ease of installation.

Cork flooring can be durable enough for use in high-traffic areas such as kitchens. Its slightly soft feel underfoot makes it an ideal surface for long periods of standing. And, if you drop a glass on it, both the glass and the floor will likely remain intact.

Palm is another fast-growing plant. Like bamboo, it lacks the strength to be used like a traditional hardwood. However, it can be processed the same way as bamboo to produce an equally hard-wearing floor covering. This plank flooring has all the warmth of hardwood, but the material is renewable.

Custom mosaic tile sheets can be created to meet just about any design scheme. Here, tempered glass tiles reflect light into interesting colors reminiscent of mother of pearl, while solid-tone ceramic tiles establish an overall color and add stability to the design.

Project Preparation

Before your new floor goes in, your old floor will probably need to be taken out and the subfloor will need to be carefully prepared for a finished surface. Project preparation is just as important as installing your floor covering and requires the same attention to detail.

Removing old floors, installing new subfloors or underlayments, and filling in cracks and joints isn't the most glamorous job in the world, but it's an investment that will reap big rewards when your flooring project is complete.

If your new floor is part of a larger home improvement project, removing the existing floor should be one of the first steps in the overall project, while installing the new floor is one of the last. All other demolition and construction should be finished in the room before the floor is installed to avoid damaging the new surface.

In this chapter:

- Tools
- Floor Covering Removal
- Underlayment Removal
- Subfloor Repair
- Joist Repair

Tools

Tools for flooring removal and surface preparation include: a power sander (A), jamb saw (B), putty knife (C), floor roller (D), circular saw (E), hammer (F), hand maul (G), reciprocating saw (H), cordless drill (I), flat-edged trowel (J), notched trowel (K), stapler (L), cat's paw (M), flat pry bar (N), heat gun (O), masonry chisel (P), crowbar (Q), nippers (R), wallboard knife (S), wood chisel (T), long-handled floor scraper (U), Phillips screwdriver (V), standard screwdriver (W), utility knife (X), and carpenter's level (Y).

A power miter saw does a fast, accurate job of cutting flooring. A 10" saw will cut flooring up to at least 6" wide in one pass. For wider floorboards, flip the workpiece to finish the cut, or invest in a sliding miter saw.

Routine cleaning tools for wood, ceramic tiles, and concrete floors (from left to right): wet mop, dry mop, broom, handheld broom with dustpan, stiff bristle push broom, fine bristle push broom. A dry mop is good for picking up dust and fine particles and may be used daily. For cleaning joints and room corners, use a small handheld broom. On smooth surfaces, use a household broom, fine bristle push broom, or canister vacuum with bare floor attachments. On rough surfaces (including outdoor or garage concrete) use a stiff bristle push broom or shop vac. Every month or so it is good to damp mop concrete or ceramic tiles.

How to Measure Your Room ▸

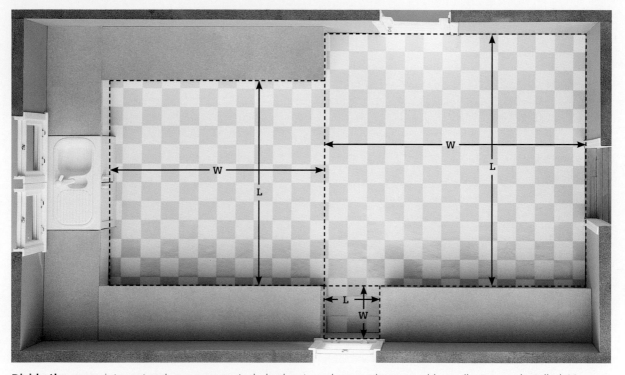

Divide the room into rectangles or squares. Include closets and areas where movable appliances are installed. Measure the length and width of each area in inches, then multiply the length times the width. Divide that number by 144 to determine the square footage.

Before ordering your floor covering, determine the total square footage of your room. To do this, divide the room into a series of squares and rectangles that you can easily measure. Be sure to include all areas that will be covered, such as closets and space under your refrigerator and other movable appliances.

Measure the length and width of each area in inches, then multiply the length times the width. Divide that number by 144 to determine the square footage. Add all of the areas together to figure the square footage for the entire room. Subtract the areas that will not be covered, such as cabinets and other permanent fixtures.

When ordering your floor covering, be sure to purchase 10 to 15% extra to allow for waste and cutting. For patterned flooring, you may need as much as 20% extra.

Floor Covering Removal

When old floor coverings must be removed, as is the case with many projects, thorough and careful removal work is essential to the quality of the new flooring installation.

The difficulty of flooring removal depends on the type of floor covering and the method that was used to install it. Carpet and perimeter-bond vinyl are generally very easy to remove, and removing vinyl tiles is also relatively simple. Full-spread sheet vinyl can be difficult to remove, however, and removing ceramic tile can be a lot of work.

With any removal project, be sure to keep your tool blades sharp, and take care not to damage the underlayment if you plan to reuse it. If you'll be replacing the underlayment, it may be easier to remove the old underlayment along with the floor covering.

Use a floor scraper to remove resilient floor coverings and to scrape off leftover adhesives or backings. The long handle provides leverage and force, and it allows you to work in a comfortable standing position. A scraper will remove most of the flooring, but you may need other tools to finish the job.

Tools & Materials ▸

Floor scraper	Eye, ear, and respiratory
Utility knife	protection
Spray bottle	End-cutting nippers
Wallboard knife	Liquid dishwashing
Wet/dry vacuum	detergent
Heat gun	Belt sander (optional)
Hand maul	Sheet plastic
Masonry chisel	Masking tape
Flat pry bar	Two-wheeler for moving
Scrap wood	large appliances
Tape measure	Screwdriver
Stapler	Wrench
Scissor	Box fan

Options for Removing Old Flooring

Remove the floor covering only. If the underlayment is sturdy and in good condition, you can usually get by with simply scraping off the floor covering, then cleaning and reusing the existing underlayment.

Remove the floor covering and underlayment. If the underlayment is questionable or substandard, or if the floor covering is bonded to the underlayment, remove the flooring and underlayment together. Taking up both layers at once saves time.

Preparing the Installation Area

Disconnect and remove all appliances. Plan out a space to store appliances temporarily while you complete your project. Be sure to position them so they are still accessible, if necessary.

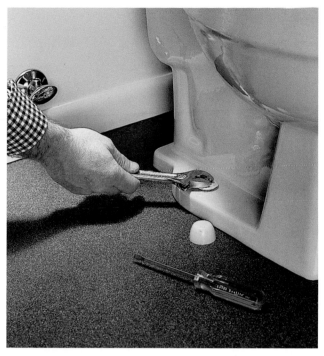

Remove the toilet and other floor-mounted fixtures before installing a bathroom floor. Turn off and disconnect the water supply line, then remove the bolts holding the toilet on the floor.

Ventilate the project room, especially when applying adhesives or removing old flooring. Placing a box fan in an open window will help draw dust and noxious fumes from the work area.

Cover entryways with sheet plastic to contain dust and debris while you remove the old floor.

(continued)

Cover heat and air vents with sheet plastic and masking tape to prevent dust and debris from entering ductwork.

Cut the paint away from the baseboard with a utility knife.

Remove the baseboard using a pry bar placed against a scrap board. Pry the baseboard at all nail locations. Number the baseboards as they are removed.

Remove the nails by pulling them through the back of the baseboard with nippers, or pliers.

How to Remove Sheet Flooring

Use a utility knife to cut the old flooring into strips about a foot wide to make removal easier.

Pull up as much flooring as possible by hand. Grip the strips close to the floor to minimize tearing.

Cut stubborn sheet vinyl into strips about 6" wide. Starting at a wall, peel up as much of the floor covering as possible. If the felt backing remains, spray a solution of water and liquid dishwashing detergent under the surface layer to help separate the backing. Use a wallboard knife to scrape up particularly stubborn patches.

Scrape up the remaining sheet vinyl and backing with a floor scraper. If necessary, spray the backing with the soap solution to loosen it. Sweep up the debris, then finish the cleanup using a wet/dry vacuum. *Tip: Add about an inch of water to the vacuum container to help control dust.*

How to Remove Resilient Tile

Starting at a loose seam, use a long-handled floor scraper to remove tiles. To remove stubborn tiles, soften the adhesive with a heat gun, then use a wallboard knife to pry up the tile and scrape off the underlying adhesive.

Remove stubborn adhesive or backing by wetting the floor with a mixture of water and liquid dishwashing detergent, then scrape it with a floor scraper.

How to Remove Ceramic Floor Tile

Knock out tile using a hand maul and masonry chisel. If possible, start in a space between tiles where the grout has loosened. Be careful when working around fragile fixtures, such as drain flanges, to prevent damage.

If you plan to reuse the underlayment, use a long-handled floor scraper to remove any remaining adhesive. You may have to use a belt sander with a coarse sanding belt to grind off stubborn adhesive.

How to Remove Carpet

Using a utility knife, cut around metal threshold strips to free the carpet. Remove the threshold strips with a flat pry bar.

Cut the carpet into pieces small enough to be easily removed. Roll up the carpet and remove it from the room, then remove the padding. *Note: Padding is often stapled to the floor and usually comes up in pieces as you roll it.*

Using end-cutting nippers or pliers, remove all of the staples from the floor. If you plan to lay new carpet, leave the tackless strips in place unless they are damaged.

Remove tackless strips immediately from the perimeter of the room. Pry them loose with a pry bar. Always wear gloves when handling tackless strips.

Variation: To remove glued-down carpet, cut it into strips with a utility knife, then pull up as much material as you can. Scrape up the remaining cushion material and adhesive with a floor scraper.

Underlayment Removal

Flooring contractors routinely remove the underlayment along with the floor covering before installing new flooring. This saves time and makes it possible to install new underlayment that's ideally suited to the new flooring. Do-it-yourselfers using this technique should make sure to cut the flooring into pieces that can be easily handled.

Warning ▸

This floor removal method releases flooring particles into the air. Be sure the flooring you are removing does not contain asbestos. See Asbestos & Flooring, page 11.

Tools & Materials ▸

Gloves
Circular saw with
   carbide-tipped
   blade
Flat pry bar
Mallet

Reciprocating saw
Wood chisel
Hammer
Dust mask
Eye and ear
   protection

Removal Tip ▸

Examine fasteners to see how the underlayment is attached. Use a screwdriver to expose the heads of the fasteners. If the underlayment has been screwed down, you'll need to remove the floor covering and then unscrew the underlayment. If the underlayment has been nailed, you can pry it up without separating the floor covering.

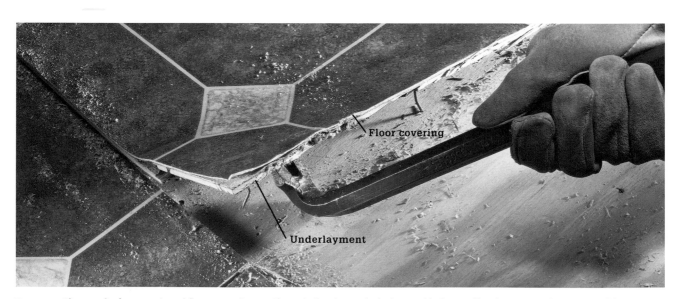

Floor covering

Underlayment

Remove the underlayment and floor covering as though they're a single layer. This is an effective removal strategy with any floor covering that's bonded to the underlayment.

How to Remove Underlayment

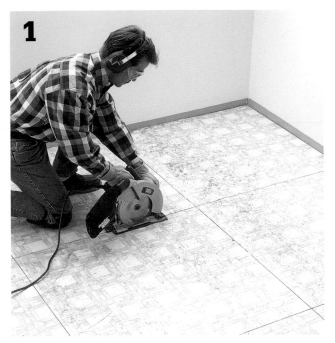

Adjust the cutting depth of a circular saw to equal the combined thickness of your floor covering and underlayment. Using a carbide-tipped blade, cut the floor covering and underlayment into squares measuring about 3 feet square. Be sure to wear safety goggles and gloves.

Use a reciprocating saw to extend the cuts to the edges of the walls. Hold the blade at a slight angle to the floor and be careful not to damage walls or cabinets. Don't cut deeper than the underlayment. Use a wood chisel to complete cuts near cabinets.

Separate the underlayment from the subfloor using a flat pry bar and hammer. Remove and discard the sections of underlayment and floor covering immediately, watching for exposed nails. If underlayment is attached to the subfloor with screws, see Tip, previous page.

Variation: If your existing floor is ceramic tile over plywood underlayment, use a hand maul and masonry chisel to chip away the tile along the cutting lines before making cuts.

Subfloor Repair

A solid, securely fastened subfloor minimizes floor movement and squeaks, and it also prevents deflection that can cause tile or groutlines to crack.

After removing the old underlayment, inspect the subfloor for loose fasteners, moisture damage, cracks, and other flaws. If your subfloor is made of dimension lumber rather than plywood, you can use plywood to patch damaged sections. If the plywood patch doesn't reach the height of the subfloor, add layers of thinner material or use floor leveler to raise the surface so it is even with the surrounding area.

Tools & Materials ▸

Flat-edged trowel	Tape measure
Straightedge	2" deck screws
Framing square	Carpenter's level
Drill	Plywood
Circular saw	2 × 4 lumber
Cat's paw	10d common nails
Wood chisel	Protective gloves
Hammer	Eye and ear protection
Floor leveler	

Subflooring that is smooth, even, and structurally sound is critical to any floor covering installation. Patch damaged areas with plywood floor panels that are the same thickness as the old subfloor.

How to Apply Floor Leveler

Floor leveler is used to fill in dips and low spots in plywood subfloors. Mix the leveler according to directions from the manufacturer, adding a latex or acrylic bonding agent for added flexibility, if specified.

Mix the leveler according to the manufacturer's directions, then spread it onto the subfloor using a trowel. Build up the leveler in thin layers to avoid overfilling the area, allowing each layer to dry before applying the next.

Use a straightedge to make sure the filled area is level with the surrounding area. If necessary, apply more leveler. Allow the leveler to dry, then shave off any ridges with the edge of a trowel, or sand it smooth.

How to Replace a Section of Subfloor

Use a framing square to mark a rectangle around the damage, making sure two sides of the rectangle are centered over floor joists. Remove nails along the lines, using a cat's paw. Make the cuts using a circular saw adjusted so the blade cuts through the subfloor only. Use a jigsaw or a chisel to complete cuts.

Remove the damaged section, then nail two 2 × 4 blocks between the joists, centered under the cut edges for added support. If possible, nail the blocks from below. Otherwise, toenail them from above, using 10d nails.

Measure the cut-out section, then cut a patch to fit. Use material that's the same thickness as the original subfloor. Fasten the patch to the joists and blocks using 2" deck screws spaced about 5" apart.

Joist Repair

A severely arched, bulged, cracked, or sagging floor joist can only get worse over time, eventually deforming the floor above it. Correcting a problem joist is an easy repair and makes a big difference in your finished floor. It's best to identify problem joists and fix them before installing your underlayment and new floor covering.

One way to fix joist problems is to fasten a few new joists next to a damaged floor joist in a process called sistering. When installing a new joist, you may need to notch the bottom edge so it can fit over the foundation or beam. If that's the case with your joists, cut the notches in the ends no deeper than one-eighth of the actual depth of the joist.

Tools & Materials ▸

4-ft. level	Circular saw	Framing lumber	Hardwood shims
Reciprocating saw	Tape measure	3" lag screws with washers	Metal jack posts
Hammer	Ratchet wrench	16d common nails	

How to Repair a Bulging Joist

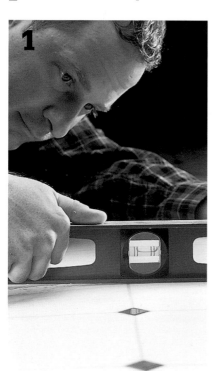

Find the high point of the bulge in the floor using a level. Mark the high point and measure the distance to a reference point that extends through the floor, such as an exterior wall or heating duct.

Use the measurement and reference point to mark the high point on the joist. Make a straight cut into the joist just below the high point mark using a reciprocating saw. Make the cut ¾ of the depth of the joist. Allow several weeks for the dead weight of the floor to cause the joist to straighten.

When the joist has settled, reinforce it by centering a board of the same width next to it. Fasten the board to the joist with 12d common nails and panel adhesive. Also drive fasteners through the joist and into the repair piece.

How to Repair a Cracked or Sagging Joist

Identify the cracked or sagging joist before it causes additional problems. Remove any blocking or bridging above the sill or beam where the sister joist will go.

Place a level on the bottom edge of the joist to determine the amount of sagging that has occurred. Cut a sister joist the same length as the damaged joist. Place it next to the damaged joist with the crown side up. If needed, notch the bottom edge of the sister joist so it fits over the foundation or beam.

Insert tapered hardwood shims at the ends of the sister joist where it sits on the sill or beam. Drive the shims in place with a hammer and scrap piece of wood until the joist is pressed firmly against the subfloor above.

Drill pairs of pilot holes in the sister joist every 12", then insert 3" lag screws with washers in each hole. Cut the blocking or bridging to fit, and install it between the joists in its original position.

Preparing the Base

New flooring succeeds or fails largely on the performance of what lies underneath. A structurally sound and level base free from imperfections will help ensure that strip floorboards and planks don't buckle or separate; that carpet and sheet flooring don't wrinkle or bubble; and that tiles don't pop.

Creating a good subbase for your flooring demands installing the appropriate underlayment. Each type of flooring has its own requirements, so be sure that you're meeting the subbase requirements of the floor covering you've selected. You'll have to balance those requirements with the surface underneath. If it's a challenging surface such as a basement floor below grade, you'll have to go through some extra steps to ensure the integrity of the underlayment and, ultimately, the floor. Most basement floors will require a vapor barrier between the concrete and the subbase.

In some situations, such as attics, you may even need to reinforce or rebuild the floor structure. The added effort will pay off in terms of comfort and security underfoot. It may be required in any case, so it's always wise to check local codes when flooring is part of a bigger remodeling project such as converting an attic into a living space.

In this chapter:

- Underlayment
- Basement Floors
- Attic Floors
- Underfloor Radiant Heat Systems

Underlayment

Underlayment is a thin layer of sheathing screwed or nailed to the subfloor to provide a smooth, stable surface for the floor covering. The type of underlayment you choose depends on the type of floor covering you plan to install. Ceramic and natural stone tile floors usually require an underlayment that stands up to moisture, such as cementboard. For vinyl flooring, use a quality-grade plywood; most warranties are void if the flooring is installed over substandard underlayments. If you want to use your old flooring as underlayment, apply an embossing leveler to prepare it for the new installation. Most wood flooring and carpeting do not require underlayment and are often placed on a plywood subfloor with only a cushion pad or rosin paper for underlayment.

When you install new underlayment, attach it securely to the subfloor in all areas, including under movable appliances. Notch the underlayment to fit the room's contours. Insert the underlayment beneath door casings and moldings. Once the underlayment is installed, use a latex patching compound to fill gaps, holes, and low spots. This compound is also used to cover screw heads, nail heads, and seams in underlayment. Some compounds include dry and wet ingredients that need to be mixed, while others are premixed. The compound is applied with a trowel or drywall knife.

¼" Plywood-AC

Fiber/cementboard

Cementboard

24 × 24" interlocking underlayment panels

Tools & Materials ▸

Drill	Floor-patching
Circular saw	compound
Drywall knife	Latex additive
Power sander	Thin-set mortar
¼" notched trowel	Fiberglass-mesh
Straightedge	wallboard tape
Utility knife	Tape measure
Jigsaw with carbide-	Eye and ear protection
tipped blade	Cementboard screws
Flooring roller	Level
Underlayment	Mallet
1" deck screws	Dust mask

How to Install Plywood Underlayment

Plywood is the most common underlayment for sheet vinyl flooring and resilient tile. For vinyl, use ¼" exterior-grade AC plywood. This type has one smooth, sanded side for a quality surface. Wood-based floor coverings, like parquet, can be installed over lower-quality plywood underlayment. When installing plywood, leave ¼" expansion gaps at the walls and between sheets. Make sure the seams in the underlayment are offset from the subfloor seams.

Install a piece of plywood along the longest wall, making sure the underlayment seams are not aligned with the subfloor seams. Fasten the plywood to the subfloor using 1" deck screws driven every 6" along the edges and at 8" intervals in the field of the sheet.

Continue fastening sheets of plywood to the subfloor, driving the screw heads slightly below the underlayment surface. Leave ¼" expansion gaps at the walls and between sheets. Offset seams in subsequent rows.

Using a circular saw or jigsaw, notch the plywood to meet the existing flooring in doorways. Fasten the notched sheets to the subfloor.

Mix floor-patching compound and latex or acrylic additive following the manufacturer's directions. Spread it over seams and screw heads using a wallboard knife.

Let the patching compound dry, then sand the patched areas using a power sander.

Installing Cementboard

Ceramic and natural stone tile floors usually require an underlayment that stands up to moisture, such as cementboard. Fiber-cementboard is a thin, high-density underlayment used under ceramic tile and vinyl flooring in situations where floor height is a concern. Cementboard is used only for ceramic tile or stone tile installations. It remains stable even when wet, so it is the best underlayment to use in areas that are likely to get wet, such as bathrooms. Cementboard is more expensive than plywood, but a good investment for a large tile installation.

Tools & Materials ▸

Cementboard	Straightedge
Thinset mortar	Notched trowel
Fiberglass drywall tape	Drill/driver
1¼" cementboard screws	Drywall knife
	Tape measure
Utility knife	Eye protection and gloves

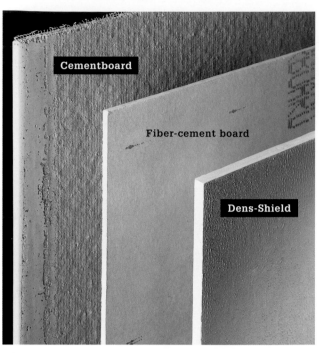

Common tile backers are cementboard, fiber-cementboard, and Dens-Shield. Cementboard is made from portland cement and sand reinforced by an outer layer of fiberglass mesh. Fiber-cement board is made similarly, but with a fiber reinforcement integrated throughout the panel. Dens-Shield is a water-resistant gypsum board with a waterproof acrylic facing.

How to Install Cementboard

Cut cementboard by scoring through the mesh just below the surface using a utility knife or carbide-tipped cutter. Snap the panel back, then cut through the back-side mesh (inset). *Note: For tile applications, the rough face of the board is the front.*

Mix thin-set mortar according to the manufacturer's directions. Starting at the longest wall, spread the mortar on the subfloor in a figure eight pattern using a ¼" notched trowel. Spread only enough mortar for one sheet at a time. Set the cementboard on the mortar with the rough side up, making sure the edges are offset from the subfloor seams.

Fasten the cementboard to the subfloor using 1¼" cementboard screws driven every 6" along the edges and 8" throughout the sheet. Drive the screw heads flush with the surface. Continue spreading mortar and installing sheets along the wall. *Option: If installing fiber-cementboard underlayment, use a ³⁄₁₆" notched trowel to spread the mortar, and drill pilot holes for all screws.*

Cut cementboard pieces as necessary, leaving an ⅛" gap at all joints and a ¼" gap along the room perimeter.

To cut holes, notches, or irregular shapes, use a jigsaw with a carbide-tipped blade. Continue installing cementboard sheets to cover the entire floor.

Place fiberglass-mesh wallboard tape over the seams. Use a wallboard knife to apply thin-set mortar to the seams, filling the gaps between sheets and spreading a thin layer of mortar over the tape. Allow the mortar to set for two days before starting the tile installation.

How to Install Cork Soundproofing Underlayment

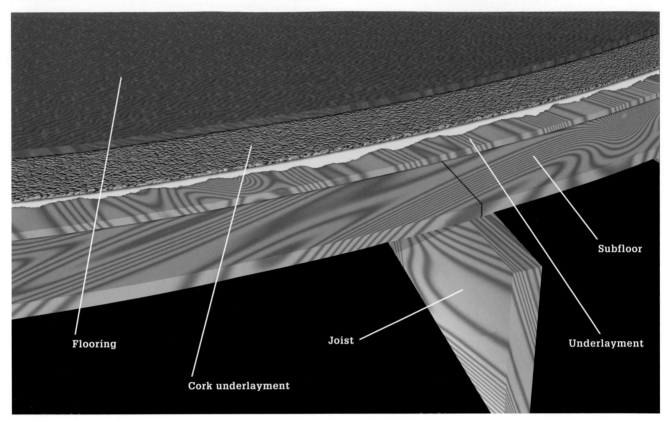

Flooring

Cork underlayment

Joist

Subfloor

Underlayment

Cork soundproofing underlayment fits between the underlayment and the floor covering. Remove floor covering, if necessary (see removal how-to steps starting on page 50).

1

Patch all holes, cracks, and joints in the plywood underlayment with cement-based patching compound using a wallboard knife. The patches must be dry and the subfloor clean before continuing.

2

Cut the cork into 2" strips using a straightedge and utility knife. Using a latex- or urethane-based adhesive, apply the strips to the base of the walls so the bottom edge sits on the floor. Press firmly to eliminate air bubbles.

3

Unroll the cork the length of the room so the curled side is face down. Butt it against the 2" strips. Be careful not to crease the cork; it's flexible enough to curl, but not to fold.

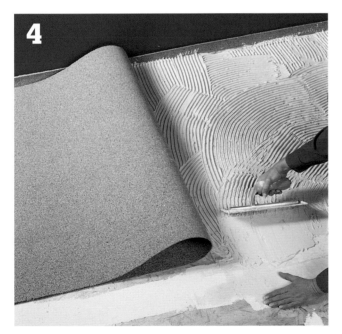

4

Pull back at least half of the roll. Apply adhesive to the plywood underlayment and spread it out, using a notched trowel. Replace the cork over the adhesive.

5

Roll the cork front to back and side to side using a floor roller. Repeat these steps to adhere the other half of the cork to the plywood underlayment. Cover the rest of the floor the same way. Butt joints tightly together, but don't overlap them.

Installing Underlayment Panels

When installing a new floor over a concrete base, raised underlayment panels that simply rest on the concrete can provide a great surface for other flooring materials. The tongue-and-groove plywood panels have dimpled plastic on the bottom. This allows air to circulate underneath so that the concrete stays dry, and insulates the flooring above. The assembled panels can support laminates, resilient sheets, or tiles. And you can install them in a weekend.

How to Install Underlayment Panels

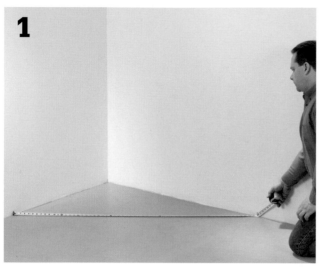

1

2

Start at one corner, and measure the length and width of the room from that starting point. Calculate the number of panels you will need to cover the space in both directions. If the starting corner is not square, trim the first row to create a straight starting line.

Create an expansion gap around the edges. Place ¼" spacers at all walls, doors, and other large obstacles. To make your own spacers, cut sheets of ¼" plywood to the thickness of the panels, and hold them in place temporarily with adhesive tape.

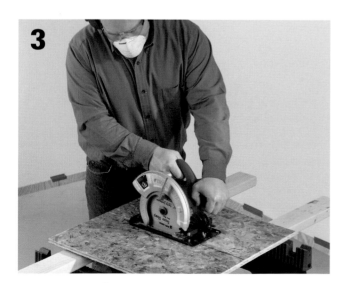

3

4

Dry-lay a row of panels across the room. If the last row will be less than 6" wide, balance it by trimming the first panel or the starting row, if necessary, to account for the row end pieces.

Starting in the corner, lay the first panel with the grooved side against the ¼" spacers. Slide the next panel into place and press-fit the groove of the second panel onto the tongue of the first. Check the edges against the wall.

Repeat these steps to complete the first row. If necessary, tap the panels into place with a scrap piece of lumber and a rubber mallet or hammer—just be careful not to damage the tongue or groove edges. Starting with the second row, stagger the seams so that the panels interlock.

Cut the last panel to fit snugly between the next-to-last panel and the ¼" spacer on the far wall. Install the last panel at an angle and tap it down. Continue working from the starting point, checking after each row to be sure the panels are square and level.

When you reach the last row and last panel to complete your installation, you may have to cut the panel to fit. Measure for fit, allowing for the ¼" expansion gap from the wall. Cut the panel and fit it into place.

When all the panels are in place, remove the spacers from around the perimeter of the room. *Note: You may choose to wait to remove the spacers until after your flooring project is finished, depending on the floor covering material.*

Basement Floors

How you prepare a concrete basement floor depends on the condition of the floor, the floor covering you plan to use, and how you want the floor to feel underfoot.

To lay flooring directly over concrete, prepare the floor to make it smooth and flat. Fill cracks, holes, and expansion joints with a vinyl- or cement-based floor-patching compound. If the concrete is especially rough or uneven, apply a self-leveling, cement-based liquid floor leveler that fills low spots and dries to form a hard, smooth surface.

For a more resilient and comfortable basement floor, build a wood subfloor to serve as a nailing surface for certain types of flooring. A subfloor does take up valuable headroom, so you may want to save space by using 1 × 4 sleepers instead of 2 × 4s. Consider how the added floor height will affect room transitions and the bottom step of the basement stairs.

Always choose a floor covering before preparing a concrete floor, solve any moisture problems before installing a new surface, and be sure to follow manufacturer recommendations for installing on concrete. Both the results and the warranty may depend on it.

Tools & Materials ▸

Vacuum	Powder-actuated nailer
Masonry chisel	Vinyl floor-patching
Hammer	compound
Trowel	Concrete primer
Floor scraper	Floor leveler
Long-nap paint roller	Pressure-treated 2 × 4s
Wheelbarrow	6-mil polyethylene
Utility knife	sheeting
Gage rake	Cedar shims
4-ft. level	Construction adhesive
Circular saw	Concrete fasteners
Caulk gun	¾" tongue-and-groove
Chalk line	plywood
Drill	2" wallboard screws
Sledgehammer	Tape measure
Packing tape	Eye and ear protection

Moisture Tip ▸

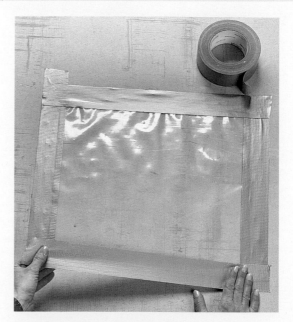

To test your floor for moisture, duct tape a 2 × 2-ft. piece of clear plastic to the concrete. Remove the plastic after 24 hours. If there's moisture on the plastic, you have a moisture problem. Do not install flooring until the problem has been fixed.

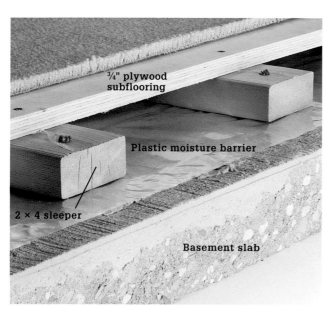

¾" plywood subflooring

Plastic moisture barrier

2 × 4 sleeper

Basement slab

Most basement floors need preparation before new flooring can be laid. Patching compound and floor leveler can smooth rough concrete, while a wood subfloor creates a new surface that feels like a framed wood floor.

How to Patch Concrete Floors

Remove any loose or flaking concrete with a masonry chisel and hammer and vacuum the floor. Mix a batch of vinyl floor-patching compound, following the manufacturer's directions. Apply the compound using a smooth trowel, slightly overfilling the cavity. Smooth the patch flush with the surrounding surface.

After the compound has cured, use a floor scraper to scrape the patched areas smooth.

How to Apply Concrete Floor Leveler

Remove any loose material and clean the concrete thoroughly so it's free of dust, dirt, oils, and paint. Apply an even layer of concrete primer to the entire surface using a long-nap paint roller. Let the primer dry completely before continuing.

Following the manufacturer's instructions, mix the floor leveler with water. The batch should be large enough to cover the entire floor area to the desired thickness (up to 1"). Pour the leveler over the floor.

Distribute the leveler evenly using a gage rake or spreader. Work quickly since the leveler begins to harden in 15 minutes. Use a trowel to feather the edges and create smooth transitions with uncovered areas. Let the leveler dry for 24 hours.

How to Build a Basement Subfloor

1

Chip away loose or protruding concrete with a masonry chisel and hammer, then vacuum the floor. Roll out strips of 6-mil polyethylene sheeting, extending them 31" up each wall. Overlap strips by 6", then seal the seams with packing tape. Temporarily tape the edges along the walls. Be careful not to damage the sheeting.

2

Lay out pressure-treated 2 × 4s along the perimeter of the room. Position the boards ½" in from all walls (inset). *Note: Before laying out the sleepers, determine where any partition walls will go. If a wall will fall between parallel sleepers, add an extra sleeper to support the planned wall.*

3

Using a circular saw, cut the sleepers to fit between the perimeter boards, leaving a ¼" gap at each end. Position the first sleeper so it is 16" from the outside edge of the perimeter board on-center. Lay out the remaining sleepers using 16"-on-center spacing.

4

Where necessary, use tapered cedar shims to compensate for dips and variations in the floor. Place a 4-ft. level across neighboring sleepers. Apply construction adhesive to two wood shims. Slide the shims under the board from opposite sides until the board is level with adjacent sleepers.

Fasten the perimeter boards and sleepers to the floor using a powder-actuated nailer or masonry screws. Drive a fastener through the center of each board at 16" intervals. Fastener heads should not protrude above the board's surface. Place a fastener at each shim location, making sure the fastener penetrates both shims.

Establish a control line for the first row of plywood sheets by measuring 49" from the wall and marking the outside sleeper at each end of the room. Snap a chalk line across the sleepers at the marks. Run a ¼"-wide bead of adhesive along the first six sleepers, stopping just short of the control line.

Position the first sheet of plywood so the end is ½" away from the wall and the grooved edge is flush with the control line. Fasten the sheet to the sleepers using 2" wallboard screws. Drive a screw every 6" along the edges and every 8" in the field. Don't drive screws along the grooved edge until the next row of sheeting is in place.

Install the remaining sheets in the first row, maintaining an ⅛" gap between ends. Begin the second row with a half-sheet (4 ft. long) so the end joints between rows are staggered. Fit the tongue of the half sheet into the groove of the adjoining sheet. If necessary, use a sledgehammer and wood block to help close the joint. After completing the second row, begin the third row with a full sheet. Alternate this pattern until the subfloor is complete.

Attic Floors

Most unfinished attic floors are merely ceiling joists and are too small to support living spaces. However, if your attic already has floor trusses (joists 2 × 8 or larger) or the same framing as the floor on your main level, it probably doesn't need additional framing.

Before you build, consult an architect, engineer, or general contractor as well as a local building inspector. Ask what size joists you'll need and which options your local building codes allow. Joist sizing is based on joist span and spacing; an attic floor must be able to support 40 pounds per square feet (psf) of live load, such as occupants and furniture, and 10 psf of dead load, such as wallboard and floor covering.

The simplest way to strengthen your attic floor is to install an additional joist next to each existing joist and nail the two together. This process, known as sistering, is done when the current joists are damaged or loose, squeak, or can't support additional weight. This method only works for joists that are 2 × 6 or larger, closely spaced, and without obstructions.

Another alternative is to build a new floor by placing larger joists between the existing ones. By resting the joists on 2 × 4 spacers, you avoid obstructions and minimize damage to the ceiling surfaces below. Be aware that the spacers will reduce your headroom by 1½ inches in addition to the depth of the joists.

Floor joist cavities offer space for concealing the plumbing, wiring, and ductwork servicing your attic, so consider these systems as you plan. Plan the locations of partition walls to determine if additional blocking between joists is necessary.

When the framing is done, the mechanical elements and insulation are in place, and everything has been inspected and approved, complete the floor by installing ¾-inch tongue-and-groove plywood. If your project will include kneewalls, you can omit the subflooring behind the kneewalls, but a complete subfloor adds strength and provides a sturdy surface for storage.

Tools & Materials ▸

Circular saw	8d common nails
Rafter square	2 × 4 lumber
Drill	¾" tongue-&-groove
Tape measure	plywood
Caulk gun	Construction adhesive
Joist lumber	2¼" wallboard screws
16d common nails	Hammer
10d common nails	

Before installing a new attic floor covering, make sure the joists are strong enough to support the weight of the new living space.

How to Add Sister Joists

Remove all insulation from the joist cavities and carefully remove any blocking or bridging between the joists. Determine the lengths for the sister joists by measuring the existing joists. Also measure the outside end of each joist to determine how much of the top corner needs to be cut away to fit the joist beneath the roof sheathing. *Note: Joists that rest on a bearing wall should overlap each other by at least 3".*

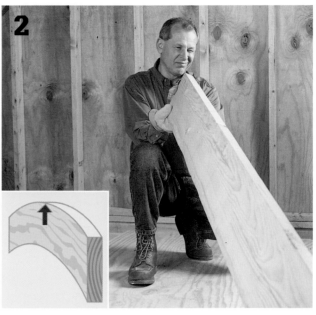

Before cutting the joists, sight down both narrow edges of each board to check for crowning, which is an upward arching along the length of the board. Draw an arrow pointing toward the arch. Joists must be installed crown side up. Cut the board to length, then clip the top outside corner to match the existing joist.

Set the sister joists in place, flush against the existing joists with their ends aligned. Toenail each sister joist to the top plates of both supporting walls using two 16d common nails.

Face-nail the joists together using 10d common nails. Drive three nails in a row, spacing the rows 12 to 16" apart. *Note: To minimize damage (such as cracking and nail popping) to the ceiling surface below, you can use a pneumatic nail gun or 3" lag screws instead of nails.* Install new blocking between the sistered joists as required by the local building code.

How to Build an Attic Floor Using New Joists

1

Remove any blocking or bridging from between the existing joists, being careful not to disturb the ceiling below. Cut 2 × 4 spacers to fit snugly between each pair of joists. Lay the spacers flat on the top plate of each supporting wall. Nail the spacers to the top plates using 16d common nails.

2

Create a layout for the new joists by measuring across the tops of existing joists and using a rafter square to transfer the measurements down to the spacers. Using 16"-on-center spacing, mark the layout along one exterior wall, then mark an identical layout on the interior bearing wall. The layout on the opposing exterior wall will be offset 11½" to account for the joist overlap at the interior wall.

3

Measure from the outer edge of the exterior wall to the far edge of the interior bearing wall. The joists must overlap above the interior wall by at least 3". Measure the outside end of each joist to determine how much of the top corner needs to be cut away to fit under the roof sheathing. Cut the joists to length, then clip the top outside corners as necessary.

4

Set the joists in place on their layout marks. Toenail the outside end of each joist to the spacer on the exterior wall using three 8d common nails.

Nail the joists together where they overlap atop the interior bearing wall using three 10d common nails for each connection. Toenail the joists to the spacers on the interior bearing wall using 8d common nails.

Install blocking or bridging between the joists, as required by your local building code. As a suggested minimum, the new joists should be blocked as close as possible to the outside ends and at the points where they overlap at the interior wall.

Installing Subflooring

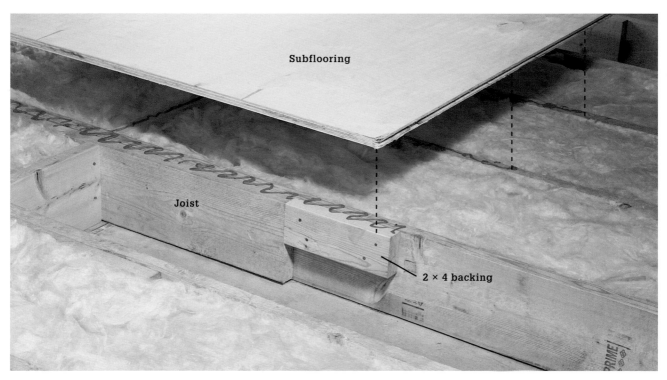

Subflooring

Joist

2 × 4 backing

Install the subfloor only after all of the framing, plumbing, wiring, and ductwork are complete and have passed the necessary building inspections. Install insulation as needed and complete any caulking necessary for soundproofing. Fasten the subflooring sheets with construction adhesive and 2¼" wallboard or deck screws, making sure the sheets are perpendicular to the joists and the end joints are staggered between rows. Where joists overlap at an interior bearing wall, add backing as needed to compensate for the offset in the layout. Nail a 2 × 4 (or wider) board to the face of each joist to support the edges of the sheets.

Underfloor Radiant Heat Systems

Floor-warming systems require very little energy to run and are designed to heat ceramic tile floors only; they generally are not used as sole heat sources for rooms.

A typical floor-warming system consists of one or more thin mats containing electric resistance wires that heat up when energized like an electric blanket. The mats are installed beneath the tile and are hardwired to a 120-volt GFCI circuit. A thermostat controls the temperature, and a timer turns the system off automatically.

The system shown in this project includes two plastic mesh mats, each with its own power lead that is wired directly to the thermostat. Radiant mats may be installed over a plywood subfloor, but if you plan to install floor tile you should put down a base of cementboard first, and then install the mats on top of the cementboard.

A crucial part of installing this system is to use a multimeter to perform several resistance checks to make sure the heating wires have not been damaged during shipping or installation.

Electrical service required for a floor-warming system is based on size. A smaller system may connect to an existing GFCI circuit, but a larger one will need a dedicated circuit; follow the manufacturer's requirements.

To order a floor-warming system, contact the manufacturer or dealer (see Resources, page 266). In most cases, you can send them plans and they'll custom-fit a system for your project area.

Tools & Materials ▸

Vacuum cleaner	Trowel or rubber float
Multimeter	Conduit
Tape measure	Thinset mortar
Scissors	Thermostat with sensor
Router/rotary tool	Junction box(es)
Marker	Tile or stone
Electric wire fault	floorcovering
indicator (optional)	Drill
Hot glue gun	Double-sided
Radiant floor mats	carpet tape
12/2 NM cable	Cable clamps

A radiant floor-warming system employs electric heating mats that are covered with floor tile to create a floor that's cozy underfoot.

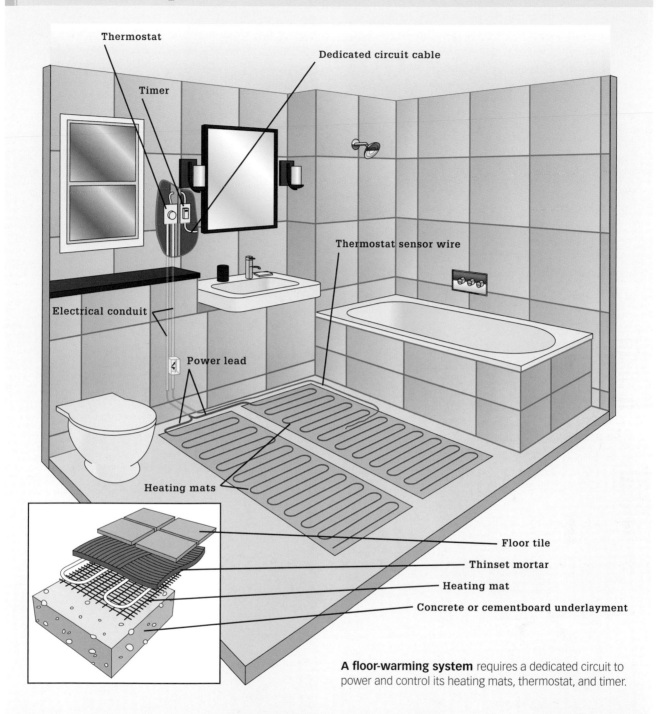

Thermostat

Timer

Dedicated circuit cable

Thermostat sensor wire

Electrical conduit

Power lead

Heating mats

Floor tile

Thinset mortar

Heating mat

Concrete or cementboard underlayment

A floor-warming system requires a dedicated circuit to power and control its heating mats, thermostat, and timer.

- Each radiant mat must have a direct connection to the power lead from the thermostat, with the connection made in a junction box in the wall cavity. Do not install mats in series.
- Do not install radiant floor mats under shower areas.
- Do not overlap mats or let them touch.
- Do not cut heating wire or damage heating wire insulation.
- The distance between wires in adjoining mats should equal the distance between wire loops measured center to center.

Installing a Radiant Floor-Warming System

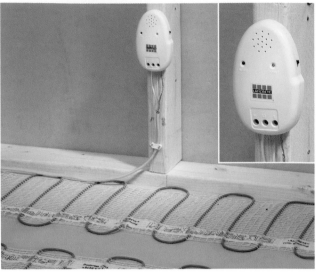

Floor-warming systems must be installed on a circuit with adequate amperage and a GFCI breaker. Smaller systems may tie into an existing circuit, but larger ones need a dedicated circuit. Follow local building and electrical codes that apply to your project.

An electric wire fault indicator monitors each floor mat for continuity during the installation process. If there is a break in continuity (for example, if a wire is cut) an alarm sounds. If you choose not to use an installation tool to monitor the mat, test for continuity frequently using a multimeter.

How To Install a Radiant Floor-Warming System

Install electrical boxes to house the thermostat and timer. In most cases, the box should be located 60" above floor level. Use a 4"-deep × 4"-wide double-gang box for the thermostat/timer control if your kit has an integral model. If your timer and thermostat are separate, install a separate single box for the timer.

Drill access holes in the sole plate for the power leads that are preattached to the mats (they should be over 10 ft. long). The leads should be connected to a supply wire from the thermostat in a junction box located in a wall near the floor and below the thermostat box. The access hole for each mat should be located directly beneath the knockout for that cable in the thermostat box. Drill through the sill plate vertically and horizontally so the holes meet in an L-shape.

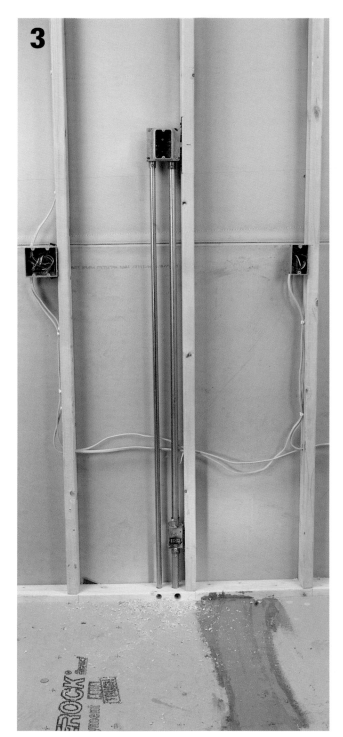

3

Run conduit from the electrical boxes to the sill plate. The line for the supply cable should be ¾" conduit. If you are installing multiple mats, the supply conduit should feed into a junction box about 6" above the sill plate and then continue into the ¾" hole you drilled for the supply leads. The sensor wire needs only ½" conduit that runs straight from the thermostat box via the thermostat. The mats should be powered by a dedicated 20-amp GFCI circuit of 12/2 NM cable run from your main service panel to the electrical box (this is for 120-volt mats—check your instruction manual for specific circuit recommendations).

4

Clean the floor surface thoroughly to get rid of any debris that could potentially damage the wire mats. A vacuum cleaner generally does a more effective job than a broom.

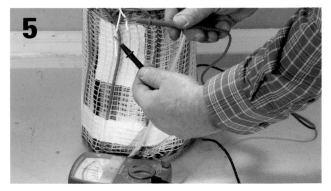

5

Test for resistance using a multimeter set to measure ohms. This is a test you should make frequently during the installation, along with checking for continuity. If the resistance is off by more than 10% from the theoretical resistance listing (see manufacturer's chart in installation instructions), contact a technical support operator for the kit manufacturer. For example, the theoretical resistance for the 1 × 50 ft. mat seen here is 19, so the ohms reading should be between 17 and 21.

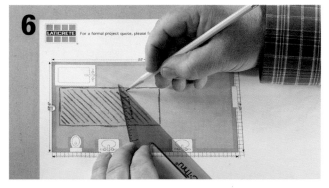

6

Finalize your mat layout plan. Most radiant floor warming mat manufacturers will provide a layout plan for you at the time of purchase, or they will give you access to an online design tool so you can come up with your own plan. This is an important step to the success of your project, and the assistance is free.

(continued)

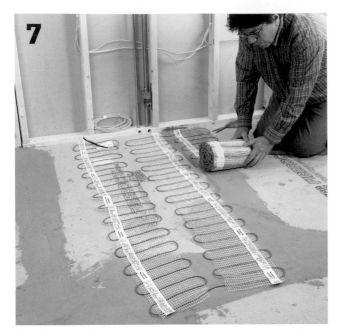

7

Unroll the radiant mat or mats and allow them to settle. Arrange the mat or mats according to the plan you created. It's okay to cut the plastic mesh so you can make curves or switchbacks, but do not cut the heating wire under any circumstances, even to shorten it.

8

Finalize the mat layout and then test the resistance again using a multimeter. Also check for continuity in several different spots. If there is a problem with any of the mats, you should identify it and correct it before proceeding with the mortar installation.

9

Run the thermostat sensor wire from the electrical box down the ½" conduit raceway and out the access hole in the sill plate. Select the best location for the thermostat sensor and mark the location onto the flooring. Also mark the locations of the wires that connect to and lead from the sensor.

Variation: If your local codes require it, roll the mats out of the way and cut a channel for the sensor and the sensor wires into the floor or floor underlayment. For most floor materials, a spiral cutting tool does a quick and neat job of this task. Remove any debris.

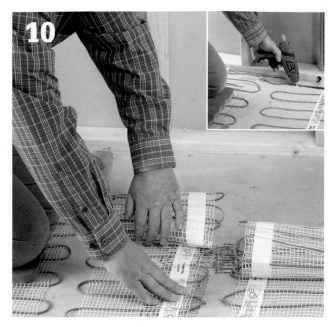

Bond the mats to the floor. If the mats in your system have adhesive strips, peel off the adhesive backing and roll out the mats in the correct position, pressing them against the floor to set the adhesive. If your mats have no adhesive, bind them with strips of double-sided carpet tape. The thermostat sensor and the power supply leads should be attached with hot glue (inset photo) and run up into their respective holes in the sill plate if you have not done this already. Test all mats for resistance and continuity.

Cover the floor installation areas with a layer of thinset mortar that is thick enough to fully encapsulate all the wires and mats (usually around ¼" in thickness). Check the wires for continuity and resistance regularly and stop working immediately if there is a drop in resistance or a failure of continuity. Allow the mortar to dry overnight.

Connect the power supply leads from the mat or mats to the NM cable coming from the thermostat inside the junction box near the sill. Power must be turned off. The power leads should be cut so about 8" of wire feeds into the box. Be sure to use cable clamps to protect the wires.

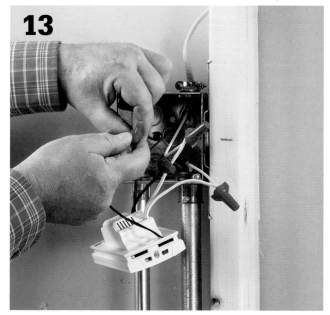

Connect the sensor wire and the power supply lead (from the junction box) to the thermostat/timer according to the manufacturer's directions. Attach the device to the electrical box, restore power, and test the system to make sure it works. Once you are convinced that it is operating properly, install floor tiles and repair the wall surfaces.

Installations

Of all the home improvements you can choose to handle yourself, flooring may be the most rewarding. You probably own and know how to use most of the tools, and the others are easy to get from rental centers. If you're concerned about your ability, take courage. Installing a floor does not require exceptional strength or skill—just planning and care.

In this chapter:

- Hardwood Floors
- Bonded Bamboo Strip Flooring
- Parquet Tiles
- Floating Laminate Floors
- Vinyl Plank Flooring
- Linoleum Tile
- Resilient Tile
- Cork Tile
- Recycled Rubber Tile
- Ceramic, Stone & Glass Tile
- Mosaic Tile
- Combination Tile
- Porcelain Snap-lock Tile
- Interlocking Utility Tile
- Bonded Rubber Roll Flooring
- Seamed Rubber Roll Flooring
- Resilient Sheet Vinyl
- Carpet
- Carpet Squares

Hardwood Floors

Wood has been a preferred flooring material since the first permanent homes were constructed. This appealing material remains a favorite in modern homes for its warmth, character, adaptability, and its unparalleled ability to age gracefully. In addition to being just plain handsome, a hardwood floor is remarkably durable; it can last many lifetimes if kept clean and it is not exposed to moisture.

The general appearance of a hardwood floor is affected by the width of the floorboards. The most common are strip floors. But wider plank floors can add a rustic charm to the right room. You can even mix it up and use boards of varying widths to create dynamic and captivating patterns across the span of a floor, but this strategy is rather tricky so you might not want to try it if you are a beginner.

Traditional strip and plank wood floors are made up of tongue-and-groove boards that are blind-nailed to a solid and level subfloor. This remains a secure, permanent way to install a wood floor. However, wood parquet floors, featuring smaller tiles of wood arranged in intricate patterns, are laid in a bed of adhesive (as are most wood floors installed on top of a concrete slab). Newer engineered wood flooring can be installed as a floating floor, with individual boards simply locked together over a padded underlayment, unattached to the subfloor or walls.

For a stunning special effect in any type of wood floor, turn to medallions, inlays, and other accents. These are all ways to create a one-of-a-kind floor sure to please the eye and the foot, and a host of manufacturers produce ready-to-install versions that are made to match the exact thickness of your particular floor.

The floor installed in the following project is a plank-style floor, but is not technically wood: it is an engineered floor made from bamboo (courtesy of Teragren Fine Bamboo Flooring, page 266). At ⅝-inch-thick and 5½ inches wide, the flooring is installed in precisely the same nail-down manner as any solid wood tongue-and-groove flooring.

Tools & Materials ▶

Circular saw with fine-tooth blade	Scrap lumber	Caulk gun	Wood putty
Tape measure	Flooring planks	Drill	Sandpaper
Chalk line	Rosin paper or 15# building paper	Nail set	Moldings
Power miter saw	Stapler	Flooring nailer (available for rent)	Finishing materials
Clamps	Hammer	Mallet	Notched trowel
Jigsaw or coping saw	Common nails	Flooring pull bar	Wood glue
Cutting guide	8d finish nails	Thresholds	Cardboard
Eye and ear protection	Flooring adhesive		Floor roller

Hardwood floors add elegance and warmth to any room, and will last many lifetimes if maintained correctly.

Tools for Installing Hardwood Floors

Power tools for hardwood flooring installation include: miter saw (A), circular saw (B), jigsaw (C), power nailer (D), cordless drill (E).

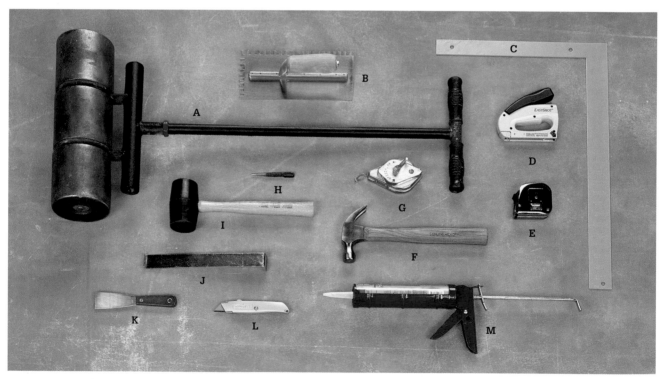

Hand tools for hardwood flooring installation include: floor roller (A), notched trowel (B), framing square (C), stapler (D), tape measure (E), hammer (F), chalk line (G), nail set (H), rubber mallet (I), floor pull bar (J), putty knife (K), utility knife (L), caulk gun (M).

Thresholds & Moldings ▸

When you install wood or laminate floors, leave a ½" gap between the perimeter of the floor and the walls to allow the wood to expand and contract with changes in temperature and humidity.

You will also have gaps that need to be covered at thresholds between rooms and around small obstacles, such as pipes. For every situation, there is a molding to fit your needs.

A floor isn't truly finished until all of the pieces are in place. These moldings help give your floors a professional look. The names for moldings may differ slightly between manufacturers.

Wood molding is used for a smooth transition between hardwood and tile in an adjoining room.

A. **Carpet reducers** are used to finish off and create a smooth transition between hard flooring and carpeting.

B. **Stair nosing** is used to cover the exposed edges of stairs where the risers meet the steps. It is also used between step-downs and landings.

C. **Baby threshold** is used in place of baseboards and quarter round in front of sliding glass doors or door thresholds, to fill the gap between the floor and door.

D. **Reducer strips,** also called transition strips, are used between rooms when the floors are at different heights and are composed of different materials.

E. **Overlap reducers** are also used between rooms when one floor is at a different height than an adjoining room.

F. **T-moldings** are used to connect two floors of equal height. They are also used in doorways and thresholds to provide a smooth transition. T-moldings do not butt up against the flooring, allowing the wood to expand and contract under it.

G. **Baseboards** are used for almost all types of floors and are available in a wide variety of designs and thicknesses. They are applied at the bottom of walls to cover the gap between the floor and walls.

H. **Quarter round,** similar to shoemolding, is installed along the bottom edge of base board and sits on top of the floor. It covers any remaining gaps between the floor and walls.

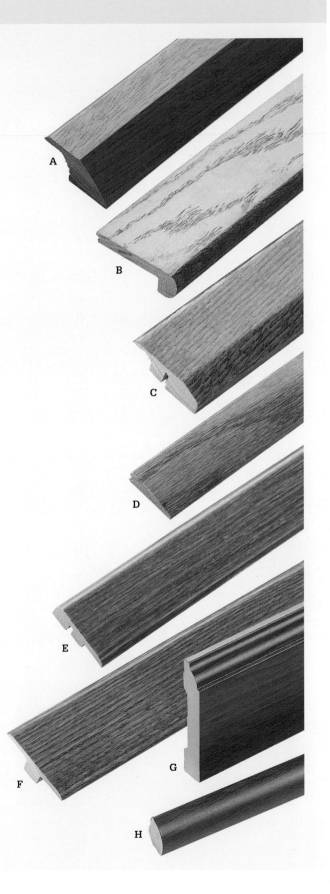

Cutting Hardwood Flooring

Ripcut hardwood planks from the back side to avoid splintering the top surface. Measure the distance from the wall to the edge of the last board installed, subtracting ½" to allow for an expansion gap. Transfer the measurement to the back of the flooring, and mark the cut with a chalk line.

When ripcutting hardwood flooring with a circular saw, place another piece of flooring next to the one marked for cutting to provide a stable surface for the foot of the saw. Clamp a cutting guide to the planks to ensure a straight cut.

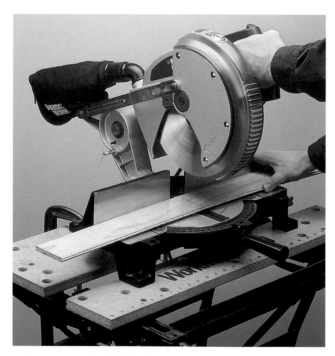

Crosscut hardwood flooring using a power miter box. Place the top surface face up to prevent splintering.

Make notched or curved cuts in hardwood flooring with a coping saw or jigsaw. If using a jigsaw, the finished surface should face down. Clamp the flooring to your work surface when cutting.

How to Install a Hardwood Plank Floor

Acclimate the flooring by stacking planks in the installation room. Separate the rows of flooring with wood scraps. Allow the material to rest in the space for several days, or as directed by the manufacturer's instructions. *Tip: Inspect your wood flooring as soon as it arrives. Look for any major defects such as knots, cracks, and damaged, warped, or bowed boards. It's easier to replace inadequate boards during the acclimation period than in mid-installation.*

Install a layer of rosin paper over the entire subfloor, stapling it down and overlapping the edges by 4". The purpose of this layer is mostly to eliminate noise caused by the floorboards scraping or pressing on the wood underlayment, which should be installed and leveled before the flooring installation begins (see pages 64 to 71).

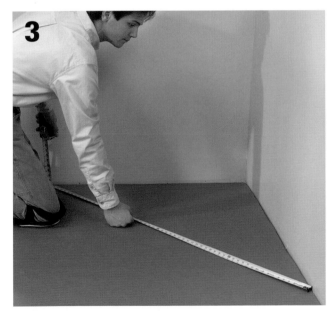

Check that the room is square using the 3-4-5 rule (measure out 3 ft. from a corner in one direction and 4 ft. in the other direction—the distance between the marks should be exactly 5 ft.). If the room is out of square, you'll have to decide which wall (usually the longest) to follow as a baseline for laying the flooring.

Determine the location of the floor joists and drive a nail in at each end, centered on the joists. Snap chalk lines along the centerlines of each joist, connecting the nails. Use these as a reference for installing floorboards.

(continued)

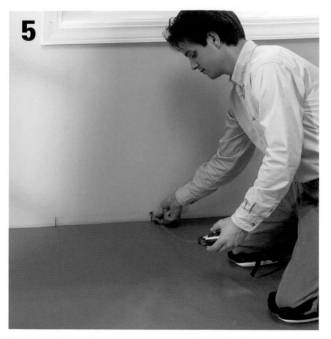

5

Snap a starter line. Measure ¾" out from the longest wall, perpendicular to the floor joists, to allow for an expansion gap. Drive a nail at each end, and snap a chalk line parallel to the wall.

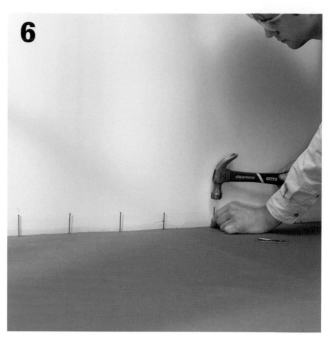

6

Drive spacer nails, such as 8d finish nails, every 4 to 5" along the chalk line, as a guide for placement of the first row of planks. Drive the nails in far enough to be stable, but with enough of the nail protruding to serve as a bumper for the flooring (and to make the nail easier to remove later).

7

Lay down a dry run for the first two or three rows to determine plank positions for best appearance. Mark the backs of planks with a pencil to keep them in your preferred order and remove them from the work area.

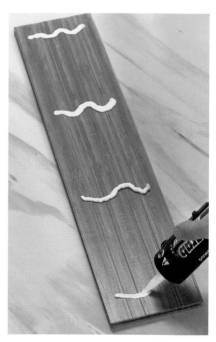

Variation: Some manufacturers recommend that you apply a bead of flooring adhesive to the backs of wider planks prior to nailing them. Use the recommended adhesive and lay beads across the width of the plank; keep adhesive at least ½" from the edges and 1½" from the ends.

8

Install the first row. Choose the longest planks available for this row. Lay the planks in place and drill holes every 8" for face nailing along the wall edge. Locate the holes ¼ to ½" in from the edge, where they'll be covered up by the base molding and shoe.

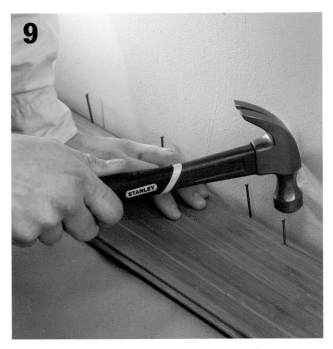

9

Attach the first floorboards by facenailing 8d finish nails into the pilot holes along the wall edge. Sink the nail heads with a nail set.

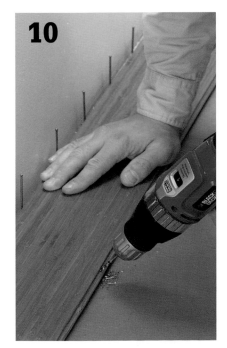

10

Pre-drill pilot holes through the tongues of the first row planks and blind nail 8d finish or flooring nails. Make sure the heads of the nails do not stick up through the tops of the tongues, where they would interfere with the tongue-and-groove joint.

Plugging Counterbores ▸

Wider plank floors frequently require that you fasten the ends of floorboards by screwing down through the board and into the subfloor. This is most commonly needed when you are installing wood flooring that does not have tongue-and-groove ends. In such cases, drill counterbored pilot holes for the screws, making sure the counterbores are deep enough to accept a wood plug. After the floorboards are installed, check to make sure the screws are tight (but be careful not to overdrive them) and then glue a wood plug into each counterbore. Wood plugs should be the same species as the flooring (or, if that's not available, make them a contrasting species). Sand the plugs so the tops are even with surrounding floor and finish them at the same time. *Note: If you are using matching plugs, orient them in the counterbores with the wood grain running parallel to the floorboards; if you are using contrasting plugs, make the grains perpendicular.*

Wood plugs and counterbore bit

(continued)

Cut the end planks for each row to length, so that the butt end faces the wall. In other words, try and preserve the tongue-and-groove profiles if your flooring has them on the ends. Saw the planks with a fine-tooth blade, making sure to orient the workpiece so you'll be cutting into the face, minimizing tearout on the surface.

After the second row, use a flooring nailer to blind-nail the tongues of each plank. Flooring nailers are struck with a mallet to drive and set the flooring nails through the floorboard tongues. They can be rented at most home centers or rental centers. *Note: You can continue to hand-nail if you choose, but be sure to continue pre-drilling pilot holes as well to avoid damaging the tongues.*

Keep joints tight. As you install each successive plank in a row, use a flooring pull bar at the open end of the plank. Drive the end of the board toward the joint by rapping on the pull bar with a mallet.

At the end of rows and along walls, use a pull bar to seat the boards. For the last row, rip the planks as necessary, use the pull bar to seat them, and facenail along the edge as you did with the first row.

If a plank is slightly bowed, cut fitting wedges to force the wayward board into position before nailing it. Make wedges by cutting two triangles from a 1 ft. or longer scrap of flooring (inset). Attach one half of the wedge pair with the outside edge parallel to the bowed plank. Slide the groove of the other wedge piece onto the tongue of the bowed plank, and hammer until the plank sits flush against its neighbor. Nail the plank into place. Remove the wedge parts.

Install a reducer strip or other transition as needed between the plank floor and adjoining rooms. Cut the strip to size and fit the strip's groove over the plank's tongue. Drill pilot holes and facenail the strip with 8d finishing nails. Sink the nails with a nail set, putty, and sand smooth.

Install a quarter-round shoe molding to cover all the expansion gaps between the floor and walls at the edge of the floor. Paint, stain or finish the molding before installing.

To reverse the direction of the tongue and groove at doorways or other openings, glue a spline into the groove of the plank. Fit the groove of the following board onto the spline and nail into place as before.

Finishing Unfinished Planks ▸

Standard strip floors are normally finished with clear or amber polyurethane finish, but the unusual look of a plank floor makes it worth considering other finishing options.

Wax is an age-old wood floor finish, one that protects the surface but needs to be renewed regularly. Wax is labor intensive, but not tricky to apply. The finish emphasizes variations in grain—a plus for many of the woods used in plank floors. It also gives the wood a deep rich glow that emphasizes the character of the species used.

Tung oil and linseed oil don't protect as well as wax, although they can be supplemented with hardeners, sealers, and other agents for a tougher finish in a range of sheens. They don't have the plastic look of polyurethane that some wood enthusiasts object to.

How to Install a Fully Bonded Wood Strip Floor

To establish a straight layout line, snap a chalk line parallel to the longest wall, about 30" from the wall. Kneel in this space to begin flooring installation.

Apply flooring adhesive to the subfloor on the other side of the layout line with a notched trowel, according to the manufacturer's directions. Take care not to obscure the layout line with adhesive.

Apply wood glue to the grooved end of each piece as you install it to help joints stay tight. Do not apply glue to the long sides of boards.

Install the first row of flooring with the edge of the tongues directly over the chalk line. Make sure end joints are tight, then wipe up any excess glue immediately. At walls, leave a ½" space to allow for expansion of the wood. This gap will be covered by moldings.

For succeeding rows, insert the tongue into the groove of the preceding row, and pivot the flooring down into the adhesive. Gently slide the tongue and groove ends together. At walls, use a hammer and a flooring pull bar to draw together the joints on the last strip (inset).

After you've installed three or four rows, use a mallet and scrap piece of flooring to gently tap boards together, closing up the seams. All joints should fit tightly.

Use a cardboard template to fit boards in irregular areas. Cut cardboard to match the space and allow for a ½" expansion gap next to the wall. Trace the template outline on a board, then cut it to fit using a jigsaw. Finish laying strips over the entire floor.

Bond the flooring to the adhesive by rolling it with a heavy floor roller. Roll the flooring within 3 hours of the adhesive application. Work in sections, and finish by installing the flooring in the section between your starting line and the wall.

A medallion made from wood strips and veneers makes a beautiful design highlight when inset into a wood floor. Flooring retailers and online flooring sellers should have access to many designs. A local craftsman can also make a custom medallion for you.

Installing a Decorative Medallion

If anything is more beautiful under your feet than a newly installed hardwood floor, it's a decorative centerpiece that complements the rest of the surface. Ready-made hardwood medallions, such as the one shown in this project, are relatively easy to install and provide a focal point for the entire room.

Tools & Materials ▸

Medallion
Installation jig
Hammer
Nails
Notched trowel
Router

Eye and ear
  protection
Pry bar
Wood putty
Urethane flooring
  adhesive

How to Install a Floor Medallion

Place the medallion on the floor where you want it installed. Draw a line around the medallion onto the floor.

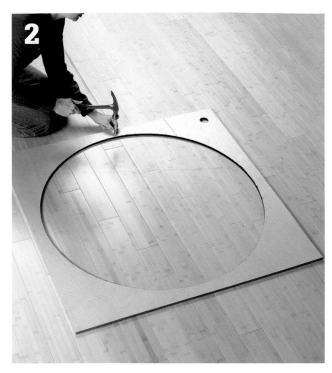

Nail the installation jig to the floor so the opening is aligned with the outline you drew in the previous step. Drive the nails into joints in the floor.

Using the router bit that came with the medallion, place the bearing of the router bit on the inside edge of the jig opening and make a ¼"-deep cut. Remove any exposed nails or staples. Make repeated passes with the router, gradually increasing the depth.

Use a pry bar to remove the flooring inside the hole. Remove all nails. Dry-fit the medallion to ensure it fits. Remove the jig and fill nail holes with wood putty.

Apply urethane flooring adhesive to the subfloor where the hardwood was removed. Spread the adhesive with a trowel. Set the medallion in place and push it firmly into the adhesive so it's level with the surrounding floor.

Bonded Bamboo Strip Flooring

It looks like hardwood, and is available in traditional tongue-and-groove form and in laminate planks. But bamboo is not wood. It's really a grass—and one of the most popular flooring materials today.

Bamboo flooring is made by shredding stalks of the raw material, then pressing them together with a resin that holds the shreds in their finished shape. Not only is bamboo a fast-growing and renewable crop, the companies that make bamboo flooring use binders with low emissions of volatile organic compounds (VOCs). The result is tough, economical, and ecologically friendly. In other words, it's just about perfect for flooring.

If you choose tongue-and-groove bamboo, the installation techniques are the same as for hardwoods. Bamboo is also available as a snap-fit laminate for use in floating floors. In this project we show Teragren Synergy Strand in Java (see Resources, 270): thin, durable planks that are glued to the underlayment.

Tools & Materials ▶

Adhesive	Moisture level meter	Bamboo flooring material	Weights
Carpenter's level	Notched trowel	Hammer	Trim
Carpenter's square	Rubber mallet	Drill	Floor leveler (if necessary)
Chalk line	Scrap lumber	Screws	Sandpaper
Cleaning supplies	Shims	Nails	Eye protection
Marking pen or pencil	Straightedge	Circular saw	and gloves
Measuring tape	Weighted roller	Butcher paper	

Tips for a Successful Installation ▶

60° 70°
RECOMENDED TEMPERATURE RANGE

40% 60%
RECOMENDED HUMIDITY RANGE

Bamboo plank flooring should be one of the last items installed on any new construction or remodeling project. All work involving water or moisture should be completed before floor installation. Room temperature and humidity of installation area should be consistent with normal, year-round living conditions for at least a week before installation. Room temperature of 60 to 70°F and a humidity range of 40 to 60% is recommended.

About radiant heat: the subfloor should never exceed 85°F. Check the manufacturer's suggested guidelines for correct water temperature inside heating pipes. Switch on the heating unit three days before flooring installation. Room temperature should not vary more than 15°F year-round. For glue-down installations, leave the heating unit on for three days following installation.

Bamboo flooring can mimic the appearance of classic hardwood, but is a much more sustainable resource that produces less harmful chemicals during the production process.

How to Install Bamboo Strip Flooring

Give the bamboo time to adjust to installation conditions. Store it for at least 72 hours in or near the room where it will be installed. Open the packages for inspection, but do not store the planks on concrete or near outside walls.

Even though thin-plank bamboo is an engineered material, it can vary in appearance. Buy all planks from the same lot and batch number. Then inspect the planks to make sure they match. Use the same lighting as you will have in the finished room.

Inspect the underlayment. Bamboo planks can be installed on plywood or oriented strand board at least ¾-inch thick. The underlayment must be structurally sound; wood surfaces should have no more than 12 percent moisture.

Make sure the underlayment is level. It should not change by more than ⅛-inch over 10 feet. If necessary, apply a floor leveler to fill any low places, and sand down any high spots. Prevent squeaks by driving screws every 6 inches into the subfloor below.

5

Sweep and vacuum the surface, then measure all room dimensions.

6

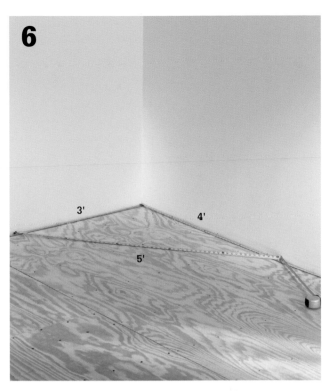

Check corners for squareness using the 3-4-5 triangle method (see page 84).

7

The planks should be perpendicular to the floor joists below. Adjust your starting point if necessary. Snap a chalk line next to the longest wall. The distance from the wall should be the same at both ends, leaving ½ inch for expansion.

8

Lay the first course of planks with the tongue edge toward the wall. Align the planks with the chalk line. Hold the edge course in place with wedges, or by nailing through the tongue edge. This row will anchor the others, so make sure it stays securely in place.

(continued)

9

Once the starter row is in place, install the planks using a premium wood flooring adhesive. Be sure to follow the manufacturer's instructions. Begin at the chalk line and apply enough adhesive to lay down one or two rows of planks. Spread the adhesive with a V-notched trowel at a 45-degree angle. Let the adhesive sit for the specified time.

10

When the adhesive is tacky and ready to use, lay the first section of bamboo planks. Set each plank in the adhesive by placing a clean piece of scrap lumber on top and tapping it down with a rubber mallet. Check the edge of each section to make sure it keeps a straight line.

11

After you finish the first section, cover the next area with adhesive and give it time to become tacky. Waiting for the adhesive to become tacky is necessary, even though it slows your work down—and it allows the section you just finished to set up.

12

When the adhesive is ready, lay down the next section of planks. Fit the new planks tightly against the previous section, taking care not to knock the finished section out of alignment. If the planks have tongue-and-groove edges, fit them carefully into place.

13

Continue applying adhesive and installing planks, one section at a time, to cover the entire floor. When adhesive gets on the flooring surface, wipe it off quickly.

14

At the edges and around any fixed objects, such as doorways or plumbing pipes, leave a ½" gap for expansion. Use shims to maintain the gaps if needed. These spaces can be covered with baseboards, base shoe, and escutcheons.

15

As you finish each section, walk across it a few times to maximize contact between the planks and the adhesive. When all the planks are in place, clean the surface and use a clean weighted roller. Push the roller in several directions, covering the entire surface many times.

16

In places that are difficult to reach with a roller, lay down a sheet of protective material, such as butcher paper, and stack weights on the paper. Let the finished floor sit for at least 24 hours, then clean the surface and remove any spacers from the expansion gaps. Finally, install the finishing trim.

Parquet Tiles

For a hardwood floor with greater design appeal, consider installing parquet. It offers more visual interest than strip flooring without sacrificing the beauty and elegance of wood. Parquet comes in a variety of patterns and styles to create geometric designs. It can range from elaborate, custom-designed patterns on the high end, to the more common herringbone pattern or the widely available and less expensive block design. The finger block pattern is one of the most widely available parquet coverings and also one of the least expensive. The configuration of perpendicular strips of wood in this design emphasizes the different grains and natural color variations.

Parquet has experienced a radical transformation over the years. A few years ago, each individual piece of parquet was hand-cut and painstakingly assembled piece by piece. Today, parquet is prefabricated so the individual pieces making up the design are available as single tiles, which has not only reduced the cost, but has made the flooring easier to install as well.

All types and designs of parquet floors are installed the same way—set in adhesive on a wood subfloor. The effort can be very rewarding: parquet can be used to create shapes and decorations not possible with other wood flooring.

Tools & Materials ▸

Tape measure	100- to 150-pound
Chalk line	floor roller
Parquet flooring	Jigsaw
Adhesive	Circular saw
Notched trowel	Paper
Putty knife	Scissors
Rubber mallet	½" spacers

Parquet is one way to add depth and pattern variety to your decor and is a great choice for both formal and casual spaces.

How to Install Parquet Flooring

Mark the centerpoint of each wall. Snap chalk lines between the marks on opposite walls to establish your reference lines. Use the 3-4-5 triangle method to check the lines for squareness (see page 93).

Lay out a dry run of panels from the center point along the reference lines to adjacent walls. If more than half of the last panel needs to be cut off, adjust the lines by half the width of the panel. Snap new working lines, if necessary.

Apply enough adhesive onto the subfloor for your first panel using a putty knife. Spread the adhesive into a thin layer with a notched trowel held at a 45° angle. Apply the adhesive right up to the working lines, but do not cover them.

Place the first panel on the adhesive so two sides are flush with the working lines. Take care not to slide or twist the panel when setting it into place. This panel must be positioned correctly to keep the rest of your floor square.

(continued)

Installations ▪ 109

Apply enough adhesive for six to eight panels and spread it with a notched trowel.

Set the next panel in place by holding it at a 45° angle and locking the tongue-and-groove joints with the first panel. Lower the panel onto the adhesive without sliding it. Install remaining panels the same way.

After every six to eight panels are installed, tap them into the adhesive with a rubber mallet.

For the last row, place a panel directly on top of the last installed row. Place a third panel on top of this, with the sides butted against ½" spacers along the wall. Draw a line along the edge of the third panels onto the second row, cut the panels at the marks, and install.

To work around corners or obstacles, align a panel over the last installed panel, then place another panel on top of it as in step 8. Keep the top panel ½" from the wall or obstacle and trace along the opposite edge onto the second panel (top). Move the top two panels to the adjoining side, making sure not to turn the top panel. Make a second mark on the panel the same way (bottom). Cut the tile with a jigsaw and install.

Within 4 hours of installing the floor, roll the floor with a 100- to 150-pound floor roller. Wait at least 24 hours before walking on the floor again.

How to Install Parquet with a Diagonal Layout

Establish perpendicular working lines following Step 1 on page 109. Measure 5 ft. from the centerpoint along each working line and make a mark. Snap chalk lines between the 5 ft. marks. Mark the centerpoint of these lines, then snap a chalk line through the marks to create a diagonal reference line.

Lay out a dry run of tiles along a diagonal line. Adjust your starting point as necessary. Lay the flooring along the diagonal line using adhesive, following the steps for installing parquet (pages 109 to 111). Make paper templates for tile along walls and in corners. Transfer the template measurements to tiles, and cut to fit.

Floating Laminate Floors

Laminate flooring is not only a handsome, less-expensive option to hardwood strips, it's also quicker and easier to install. Laminate planks (or tiles or panels) are laid as a "floating" floor; the individual tongue-and-groove units are locked together mechanically, but are not attached to walls or subfloor. There's no need for nailing, and the floor can be laid over just about any clean, level surface, including a plywood subfloor, a hardwood floor, linoleum or vinyl, or even concrete.

Although the vast majority of laminate floors are simple snap-together versions, a few manufacturers require the pieces to be glued together. Gluing is also necessary where you're concerned about moisture. In any case, the installation process is well within the abilities of even a relatively inexperienced homeowner. With the right tools, you should able to install a sizable floor easily in a single weekend. The process can be made even faster with a floating floor installation kit, available at most large home centers.

Floating floors require a shock-absorbing pad, similar to a carpet pad. You can purchase thin,

closed-cell foam pads in 100-square-foot rolls and install them as you would any other type of flooring underlayment: usually by laying out long strips and taping the seams together. High-quality laminate flooring usually has the pad preattached to each strip, panel, or plank. This simplifies installation and prevents the pad from bunching or separating.

Tools & Materials ▸

Circular saw	Vacuum
Chisel	Utility knife or scissors
Underlayment	Table saw
Rubber mallet	Finish nails
Spacers	Hammer
Tapping block	Flush cutting saw
Pull bar	Eye and ear protection
Speed square	Soft cloth
Tape measure	Drill
Tape	

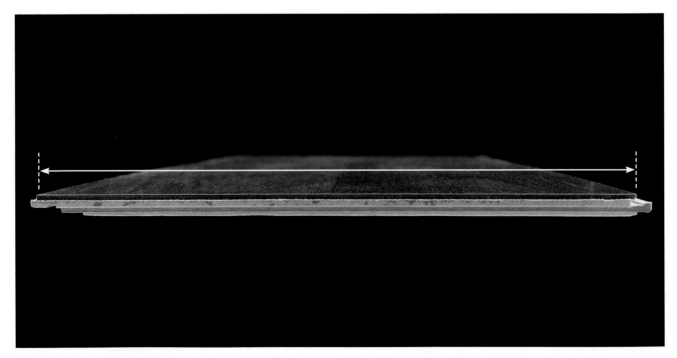

Measure from edge to edge on the top surface of the floorboard to find its actual width. Do not include the tongue in the width measurement.

Floating laminate flooring does not require adhesives or extensive fasteners, and is a great choice when installing a new floor on top of old flooring material, such as linoleum or hardwood.

How to Install a Floating Floor

Plan your layout. In most cases, you'll need to trim one row of floorboards for width so the flooring fits into the room with the correct expansion gaps between it and the wall. Measure the width of the flooring installation area and subtract ½". Divide this distance by the actual width of a plank. If the leftover amount is more than one-half of a plank width, trim the planks for your first course to that width. If it is less than one-half, add the amount to the plank width, divide by two, and trim the planks in both the first and last rows to this width.

Clear out the installation room completely and vacuum the floor thoroughly to get rid of any debris that might interfere with the installation. A vacuum cleaner is the best tool for this.

Option: Install underlayment if the product you're installing doesn't have the pad preattached. Roll out underlayment pad from the starting corner to the opposite wall. Cut the pad to fit using a utility knife or scissors. Some manufacturers recommend overlapping the rows by 2 to 3". Otherwise, butt the seams together. Tape seams with 2 or 3" clear or duct tape. Smooth sheets out as you work.

Blade guard removed for clarity

Trim the tongues off the edges of the floorboards in the first course. If you need to trim the boards for width this can be done in the same cut. Check your manufacturer's instructions first: some recommend installing the boards with the groove side facing the wall.

Set spacers against the wall around the perimeter of the installation area. Spacers are ¼ to ½" thick. If you are installing the flooring over a wood subbase you can drive finish nails ¼" away from the walls to create stops. The point of the spacers is to create an expansion gap between the flooring and the wall. *Tip: Buy an installation kit (inset) to make laying your laminate flooring an easier job. A typical kit contains a pull bar, a tapping block, and a selection of spacers.*

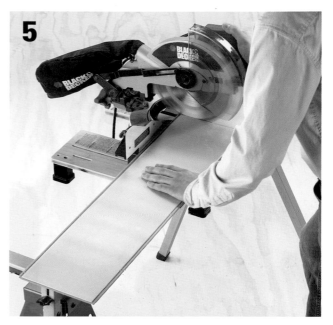

Cross-cut a floorboard into a ⅔-length piece and a ⅓-length piece to start the second and third courses, respectively. Install the floorboards so the uncut edge with the tongue or groove intact will fit with the second board in the course. Alternating the length of the first board in each course will ensure that the butt joints where floorboard ends meet do not align from course to course.

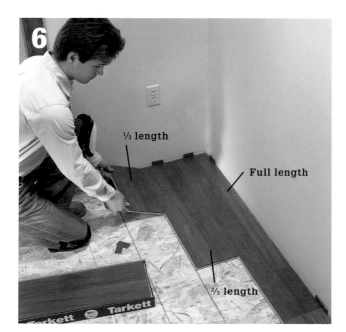

Lay the first floorboard (use a full-length board) in the farthest corner of the installation. Make sure spacers are in place so there is a gap of approximately ¼" at each corner wall. Snap a ⅔-length floorboard next to it, and a ⅓-length next to that. This will establish a repeating pattern with a ⅓-length offset between all board ends.

Fill out the first three courses and then repeat the installation sequence to fill out the entire floor area. Mark the final board in each row for cutting by placing it upside down (tongue toward wall) on the previous plank. Push it flush to the spacer on the end wall. Line up a speed square with the bottom plank edge and trace the cut line.

(continued)

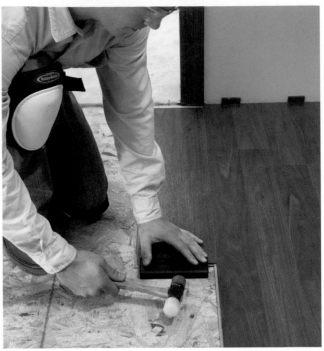

Work around door thresholds. At door openings, cut the bottoms of the door casing with a flush cutting saw to provide clearance for the flooring (left photo). When you reach the door as you lay floorboards, drive the flooring board that meets the door underneath the trimmed casing. Use a block and mallet to drive the board so the end is flush against the wall underneath the casing (right photo).

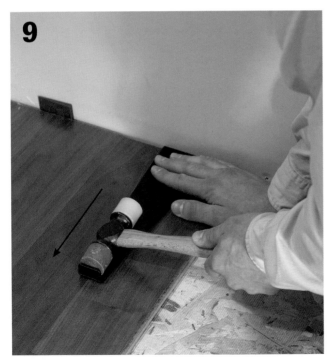

To fit the end plank for the row tightly into position, wedge one end of the pull bar between the spacer and the outside end of the plank. Tap the opposite end of the pull bar with a rubber mallet.

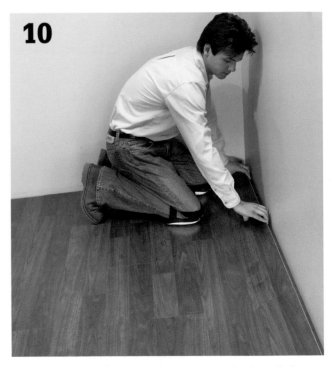

Finish installing floorboards. Rip-cut the floorboards for width if necessary (see next page). Test-fit the pieces in the last course and, if necessary, make adjustment cuts to fit using a utility knife. Finally, snap and lock the last course into place and remove all spacers. Work around obstacles as you go. Add transitions as needed.

Cutting Laminate Flooring

Rip-cut floorboards with a circular saw or table saw equipped with a fine-toothed, carbide-tipped wood blade. In either case, cut on the back side of the plank and make sure the board is clamped securely to a worksurface (when cutting with a circular saw). Cut along the waste side of the marked cut line. Use a straightedge as a guide, as shown.

Make internal cutouts with a jigsaw. If you're experienced with using power tools you can make a plunge cut with the saw blade, but to be on the safe side drill a starter hole near one corner and then make your cutout.

How to Mark for Cutting Around Obstacles

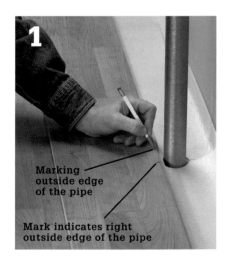

Marking outside edge of the pipe

Mark indicates right outside edge of the pipe

Position a plank end against the spacers on the wall next to the obstacle. Use a pencil to make two marks along the length of the plank, indicating the points where the obstacle begins and ends.

Once the plank is snapped into the previous row, position the plank end against the obstacle. Make two marks with a pencil, this time on the end of the plank to indicate where the obstacle falls along the width of the board.

Use a speed square to extend the four lines. The space at which they intersect is the part of the plank that needs to be removed to make room for the obstacle to go through it. Use a drill with a Forstner bit, or a hole saw the same diameter as the space within the intersecting lines, and drill through the plank at the X. You'll be left with a hole; extend the cut to the edges with a jigsaw.

Vinyl Plank Flooring

Vinyl has long been used as an alternative to linoleum and hard tiles in the kitchen and bathroom. The latest version of this adaptable material—vinyl plank flooring—combines the appeal of a hardwood floor with the easy installation and forgiving texture of a resilient material.

This unique and forgiving flooring option can be installed over just about any subfloor, as long as it is level and free of obstructions. The actual installation takes a fraction of the time required for most other floors and requires little experience.

The installation is made so easy by virtue of the planks' construction. A patterned top layer photographically produced to mimic the appearance of wood grain is bonded to a flexible base. The two layers are offset, creating a top and bottom "grip strip" on opposite edges of the plank. Once installed with the grip strips correctly interlocked, the floor is virtually waterproof.

It's also quiet, soft and warm underfoot—all of which make it an ideal option for an unusual bathroom floor in place of the more common tile. Of course, you don't need to be limited by its waterproof nature; a vinyl plank floor will add to the beauty of the home in many different rooms.

Tools & Materials ▸

Floor leveler	Tape measure
Straightedge	Spreader
Utility knife	Speed square
Floor roller	

Vinyl flooring planks are a relatively new flooring option that combines the appearance of wood strip or plank flooring with the moisture resistance of resilient flooring.

Installing Vinyl Planks

The grip strips attached to the vinyl planks are coated with an adhesive that activates as the product is warmed. If you are installing a vinyl plank floor in a room that is relatively cold, it helps to heat the seams with a heat gun or a hair dryer and roll them with a J-roller immediately after you form them. This helps activate the adhesive and creates a tighter bond between planks.

Store planks in their boxes in the room in which they'll be installed (at least 65 degrees) for 24 to 48 hours before installation. For the flooring to acclimate properly, the room temperature and the anticipated conditions should be the same as after the flooring is installed.

Vinyl plank flooring is a two-ply product with adhesive strips that overlap in the seam areas where two planks meet. Both the underside of the top ply and the top of the bottom ply are treated with adhesive, forming a near-impervious bond that sets permanently after a very brief window of time to make adjustments.

Purchase self-leveling floor underlayment to fill in any dips in the floor being covered. Even very small low areas will telegraph through the vinyl planks because they are so thin. Levelers differ somewhat from product to product, so read the label carefully to make sure the product you buy is suitable for your application and that you have all the materials you need. The product above, for example, is specially formulated for glue-down floors and requires a primer that's purchased separately.

How to Install Vinyl Plank Flooring

Measure the length and width of the room to determine square footage. Measure alcoves, bumpouts, and other areas separately. Add 10% to the total square footage when ordering the floor. While measuring, check that the room is square by measuring the length of the room at different points along two walls.

Apply floor leveler (see page 119) to fill large cracks, deep grout lines, dips, holes, or other irregularities in the subfloor before installing planks. Use an appropriate floor leveler product for the particular subfloor material.

Beginning along the longest wall, lay out the first row of planks without connecting them. Mark the end plank for cutting by setting it down backwards and upside-down on the previous plank in the row. The top attachment strip should be facing away from the wall. Mark the back of the plank and cut with a utility knife and straightedge.

Begin laying planks using ⅛" spacers to maintain uniform expansion gaps between the row and the wall. Lay planks so that the bottom attachment strip is on the opposite side of the wall edge. Trim the top strip from the wall side before laying planks.

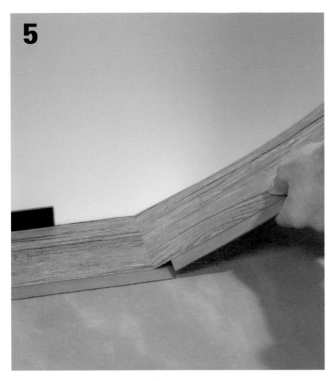

Attach planks in the row by rolling the top attachment strip of the new plank at a 45° angle into the bottom attachment strip of the preceding plank. Work slowly and carefully and make sure the seams are tight.

Cut planks as necessary by marking the top of the plank, scoring with a utility knife equipped with a new, sharp blade, and snapping off the waste section.

Stagger the planks. Start the second row by cutting a plank ⅔ of the length of the first plank in the starter row. Start the third row with a ⅓ length plank. Continue this pattern throughout the rows.

Roll the seams. Immediately after you finish laying the floor, use a weighted floor roller to roll all the seams between planks. The floor is ready to be walked on as soon as it has been rolled.

Linoleum Tile

Like sheet linoleum, linoleum tile is a natural floor covering produced from sustainable resources that include linseed oil, pine resin, and other organic additives. These ingredients make for an exceptionally green floor covering with little or no negative impact in air quality in your home. Linoleum is also anti-static and has antimicrobial properties that inhibit the growth of germs and harmful microorganisms.

Although linoleum is still offered as sheet flooring, the far easier option to install is linoleum tile in the form of "click" panels, such as the Marmoleum product seen here (see Resources, page 266). These tiles are comprised of a linoleum surface bonded over moisture-resistant, high-density fiberboard. A cork layer also adds a comfortable feel underfoot and dampens sound transmission. The flooring is available in 12-inch square tiles and panels sized at 12 inches by 36 inches.

These formats—and a noteworthy palette of available colors—give you a great deal of flexibility in designing a floor to fit your décor. Although the moisture-resistant nature of linoleum tile makes it a great choice for kitchens and baths, the dusky colors, appealing finish, and comfortable, warm feel make it appropriate for just about any room or décor. The tiles and panels can be mixed and matched to create a complex pattern of shapes and shades, or you can use one or the other to create a floor design that's more restful visually.

No matter what colors or design you choose, installing a linoleum click floor is an easy process. The panels can be installed over any clean, dry, structurally sound surface with no more than $\frac{3}{32}$-inch of height variation per six feet of surface. The panels are simply snapped together row by row. And because the process uses no glue or adhesive, the floor can be walked on as soon as you're done installing it.

Tools & Materials ▸

Circular saw, jigsaw or handsaw	Eye and ear protection	Speed square	Glue
	⅜" spacers	Wedge	Tape measure
Clamps	Linoleum click tiles	2 × 4 scrap lumber	

Click-together planks with linoleum for the top layer make striped floor patterns very easy to create. You can choose two colors to alternate, or several colors, preferably within a single family of tones.

Visually, this floor features the soft, natural beauty of linoleum. But where sheets of linoleum typically require a professional installer, the click-together tiles used here are as easy to install as any laminate flooring made for DIYers.

Installing Linoleum Tiles or Strips

1

Prepare the subfloor and the flooring. Ensure that the subfloor surface is clean and free of protrusions. Remove tiles or panels from the box and inspect each one for damage. Choose the first panel or tile in the starter row and saw off the tongue from the sides that will butt against walls. Make sure the workpiece is clamped securely and use a circular saw, jigsaw, or handsaw to trim off the tongues.

2

Position the first panel or tile in the corner of the longest wall (preferably opposite to the largest window in the room), positioning the sides from which the tongue has been removed against the walls. Use ⅜" spacers to maintain an expansion gap between the panels and the walls.

3

Position the tongue end of the second panel or tile inside the groove in the first, with the far end raised about 30°. Lower the raised end to lock the second panel into the first. Continue installing the row in this fashion, positioning two spacers evenly along the length of each panel.

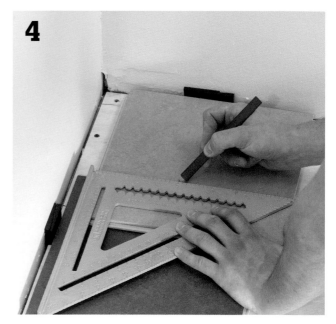

4

Measure the last panel or tile in the row for cutting by placing it on top of the preceding panel and butting it to the corner walls. The end panel should be marked on the top side (linoleum surface), with the groove side facing the wall. This is to ensure that the tongue of the end panel piece matches the preceding panel's groove. Click the end panel into place.

Begin the second row. Set the edge tongue on the preceding row's lip. Slide the wedge under the tile. Connect the next tile in the row to the first tile, set on the preceding row's lip, and slide the wedge under the strip.

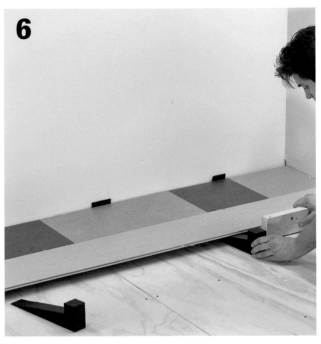

Continue connecting second-row panels or tiles to each other until you have completed the row. Slide wedges out from underneath the row. Use a 2 × 4 scrap piece to brace against the second row edges and push the entire row forward to engage with the lips on the first row's panels. Lower the second row to lock the rows together.

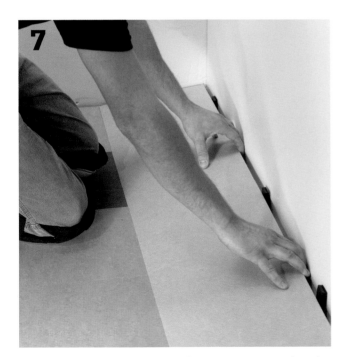

Install the remaining rows in the same manner, changing the measurement of the first panel in each row by 12" from the preceding row if you are installing strip panels. Measure, mark, and rip the pieces in the final row, using a circular saw and cutting on the faces of the pieces to prevent tearout. The final row is installed in the same way as previous rows.

Door Casings ▸

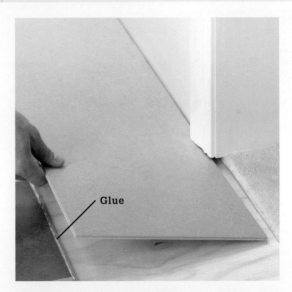

Glue

Where final panels must slide under door casings or other obstructions, remove the locking ridge from the groove side of the previous row. Lay a bead of glue along the modified groove. Slide the final row panel into place under the obstruction and pull it back snug against the glue-coated groove.

Resilient Tile

As with any tile installation, resilient tile requires carefully positioned layout lines. Before committing to any layout and applying tile, conduct a dry run to identify potential problems.

Keep in mind the difference between reference lines (see opposite page) and layout lines. Reference lines mark the center of the room and divide it into quadrants. If the tiles don't lay out symmetrically along these lines, you'll need to adjust them slightly, creating layout lines. Once layout lines are established, installing the tile is a fairly quick process. Be sure to keep joints between the tiles tight and lay the tiles square.

Tiles with an obvious grain pattern can be laid so the grain of each tile is oriented identically throughout the installation. You can also use the quarter-turn method, in which each tile has its pattern grain running perpendicular to that of adjacent tiles. Whichever method you choose, be sure to be consistent throughout the project.

Tools & Materials ▸

Tape measure	Resilient tile
Chalk line	Flooring adhesive
Framing square	(for dry-back tile)
Utility knife	1/8" spacer
1/16" notched trowel	Threshold material
Heat gun	(if necessary)

Resilient tiles have a pattern layer that is bonded to a vinyl base and coated with a transparent wear layer. Some come with adhesive pre-applied and covered by a paper backing, others have dry backs and are designed to be set into flooring adhesive.

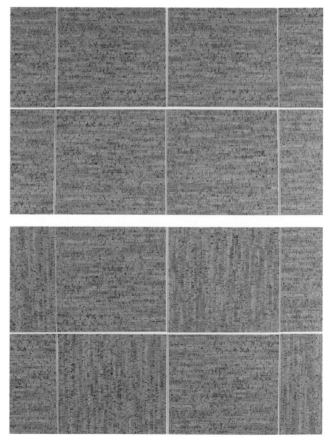

Check for noticeable directional features, like the grain of the vinyl particles. You can set the tiles in a running pattern so the directional feature runs in the same direction (top), or in a checkerboard pattern using the quarter-turn method (bottom).

How to Make Reference Lines for Tile Installation

Position a reference line (X) by measuring along opposite sides of the room and marking the center of each side. Snap a chalk line between these marks.

Measure and mark the centerpoint of the chalk line. From this point, use a framing square to establish a second reference line perpendicular to the first one. Snap the second line (Y) across the room.

Check the reference lines for squareness using the 3-4-5 triangle method. Measure along reference line X and make a mark 3 ft. from the centerpoint. Measure from the centerpoint along reference line Y and make a mark at 4 ft.

Measure the distance between the marks. If the reference lines are perpendicular, the distance will measure exactly 5 ft. If not, adjust the reference lines until they're exactly perpendicular to each other.

How to Install Dry-backed Resilient Tile

Snap perpendicular reference lines with a chalk line (see previous page). Dry-fit tiles along layout line Y so a joint falls along reference line X. If necessary, shift the layout to make the layout symmetrical or to reduce the number of tiles that need to be cut.

If you shift the tile layout, create a new line that is parallel to reference line X and runs through a tile joint near line X. The new line, X1, is the line you'll use when installing the tile. Use a different colored chalk to distinguish between lines.

Dry-fit tiles along the new line, X1. If necessary, adjust the layout line as in steps 1 and 2.

If you adjusted the layout along X1, measure and make a new layout line, Y1, that's parallel to reference line Y and runs through a tile joint. Y1 will form the second layout line you'll use during installation.

5

Apply adhesive around the intersection of the layout lines using a trowel with 1/16" V-shaped notches. Hold the trowel at a 45° angle and spread adhesive evenly over the surface.

6

Spread adhesive over most of the installation area, covering three quadrants. Allow the adhesive to set according to the manufacturer's instructions, then begin to install the tile at the intersection of the layout lines. You can kneel on installed tiles to lay additional tiles.

7

When the first three quadrants are completely tiled, spread adhesive over the remaining quadrant, then finish setting the tile.

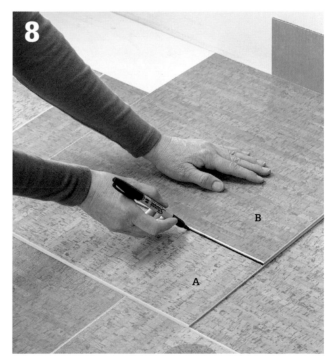

8

To cut tiles to fit along the walls, place the tile to be cut (A) face up on top of the last full tile you installed. Position a 1/8"-thick spacer against the wall, then set a marker tile (B) on top of the tile to be cut. Trace along the edge of the marker tile to draw a cutting line.

(continued)

Outside Corners ▶

To mark tiles for cutting around outside corners, make a cardboard template to match the space, keeping a ⅛" gap along the walls. After cutting the template, check to make sure it fits. Place the template on a tile and trace its outline.

9

Cut tile to fit using a ceramic-tile cutter to make straight cuts. You may use a straightedge guide and utility knife instead.

10

Install cut tiles next to the walls. If you're precutting all tiles before installing them, measure the distance between the wall and install tiles at various points in case the distance changes.

11

Check the entire floor. If you find loose areas, press down on the tiles to bond them to the underlayment. Install metal threshold bars at room borders where the new floor joins another floor covering.

How to Install Self-adhesive Resilient Tile

Once your reference lines are established, peel off the paper backing and install the first tile in one of the corners formed by the intersecting layout lines. Lay three or more tiles along each layout line in the quadrant.

Rub the entire surface of each tile to thoroughly bond the adhesive to the underlayment. Begin installing tiles in the interior area of the quadrant. Keep the joints tight between tiles.

Finish setting full tiles in the first quadrant, then set the full tiles in an adjacent quadrant. Set the tiles along the layout lines first, then fill in the interior tiles.

Continue installing the tile in the remaining quadrants until the room is completely covered. Check the entire floor. If you find loose areas, press down on the tiles to bond them to the underlayment. Install metal threshold bars at room borders where the new floor joins another floor covering.

Cork Tile

Cork flooring has all kinds of benefits. It dampens sound, resists static, insulates surfaces, and provides visual warmth like no other floor covering. Cork is a renewable natural product—tree bark—that can be harvested once a decade without cutting down the tree.

Natural cork tiles complement most furnishings and decorations, and can be found in every shade from honey yellow to deep espresso brown. Left in its original color or stained, cork has beautiful patterns that range from burls to spalting. Every tile is different, which means no two installations will look the same.

The tiles may seem fragile, but they take on the strength of the underlayment below. In fact, once a cork floor is installed and properly sealed, it can withstand normal household use just as well as any other material.

Tools & Materials ▸

Tape measure
Chalk line
Utility knife
Cork tile
Notched trowel

Scrap lumber
Rubber mallet
Joint sealer
Sander

Paint roller and tray
Recommended flooring adhesive
Level
Straightedge

Eye protection
Paper
Vacuum
Floor roller

Tips for a Successful Installation ▸

Before you work with any cork flooring material, remove it from the package and leave it in the room where it will be installed. This lets the material adjust to the room's temperature and humidity. Manufacturers recommend acclimating cork for at least 72 hours.

Cork is a renewable material that is comfortable underfoot and dampens sound. Cork is also available in many shades and has a striking natural texture.

How to Install Cork Tile

If you plan to install the cork on plywood underlayment or a similar material, make sure the surface is clean and dry, with no more change in level than ⅛" over 10 ft. Fill any low spots and sand down any high spots.

Measure the outside edges of the room, and snap chalk lines across the center. Dry-lay a row of tiles from the center to each wall.

If the last row will be less than ¼ the width of one tile, adjust the center point to balance the layout.

Apply a recommended adhesive, using the method specified by the manufacturer. Some adhesives are best applied with a paint roller, others with a notched trowel. Put down only as much adhesive as you can use in the time allowed.

Cork adhesive needs to set for 20 to 30 minutes before you can begin laying the cork tiles. After that, the working time is roughly one hour. Check the setting time specified by the adhesive manufacturer.

Begin at the intersection of the two center guidelines, and set the first tile in place. Check to make sure the adhesive holds it firmly. Continue laying tiles in the first quadrant along your layout lines.

(continued)

7

Fill in the first quadrant, one tile at a time, working from the row laid next to the layout lines. Cork tile colors and patterns will vary. Use this to your advantage by mixing batches for greater variety.

8

To fit each new tile in place, hold a piece of scrap lumber against the edge and tap it gently with a rubber mallet. If the humidity is high during installation, fit the tiles together tightly so they won't pull apart in drier weather.

9

As you complete each row, check to see that all edges are straight. If a row has gone out of line, remove as many tiles as necessary and start again. It's frustrating to make corrections now, but it's difficult or impossible later.

10

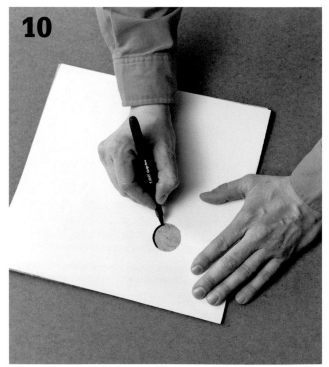

To fit tile around an object, such as a pipe or drain, cut a tile-sized piece of paper. Work the paper into the space, cutting as needed until it fits. Then lay the paper on a tile and use it as a cutting guide. Cut tiles with a utility knife.

Like other natural materials, cork will expand and contract as the temperature and humidity change. To allow space for varying conditions, leave a ¼-inch gap between the finished floor and all walls, thresholds, water pipes, and other vertical surfaces.

If your cork floor measures more than 30 feet in any direction, install a ⅝"-wide expansion joint—either in a continuous surface or where the cork meets another flooring material. This allows the cork to flex with changing conditions.

Once all the tiles are in place, vacuum the surface to remove all dust. Make several passes across the entire surface with a 100-pound floor roller. Move the roller in different directions to press every tile down securely. Let the finished floor sit overnight, then roll it again.

After rolling the surface, clean it once more and apply a recommended sealer. The most common is a water-based polyurethane. Make sure the sealer penetrates all joints so it prevents moisture from entering and damaging the finished floor. Allow the sealed floor to cure for another day before you use it. Install molding, trim, and other finishing pieces.

Recycled Rubber Tile

You see it everywhere, though you might not recognize it, in commercial buildings from office towers to skating rinks. Sometimes it's solid black, but most often it has one or two other colors blended in as small flecks. It's recycled rubber made from ground-up tires. And these days, more people than ever are installing it in their homes.

In basements, it takes the chill out of a concrete floor, making laundry rooms and workshops more pleasant places to spend time. In mudrooms and breezeways, it stands up to heavy traffic and messy conditions. It doesn't work quite as well in kitchens, because recycled rubber tends to be porous, which means it can soak up grease and oil. A rubber kitchen floor would quickly become slippery and might develop unpleasant odors.

If you want flooring that resists changing weather conditions, withstands heavy traffic, and helps keep materials out of the waste stream, recycled rubber is an ideal choice.

Tools & Materials ▸

Adhesive
Butcher paper
  for template
Carpenter's square
Chalk line
Cleaning supplies
Utility knife
Flat-edged trowel
Marking pen
  or pencil
Measuring tape
Mineral spirits
Notched trowel
Painter's tape

Shims
Weighted floor roller
Level
Floor leveler
Power sander
Rubber tiles
Hand roller
Weights
Trim pieces
Eye protection

Recycled rubber tiles are a great solution for lots of indoor rooms, such as workshops, laundry, or utility rooms. The material is durable and comfortable, and helps keep waste rubber out of our landfills.

How to Install Recycled Rubber Tile

If you plan to install rubber tile on plywood underlayment or a similar material, the surface must be level, with no more change than ⅛" over 10 ft. Fill any low spots.

Sand down high spots. Make sure the underlayment is clean, smooth, and securely fastened to the subfloor. Check the manufacturer's instructions to be sure the recommended adhesive will work with your underlayment.

To allow space for changes in temperature and humidity, leave a ¼" gap between the finished floor and all walls, thresholds, water pipes, and other vertical surfaces.

Measure the length and width of the room to be covered. Find the center of each direction and snap a chalk line across the room. The intersection of these lines is the middle of the room. Check the lines for square using the 3-4-5 method.

Dry-lay a row of tiles in each direction until you reach all four walls. If the last tile needs to be cut narrower than ¼ the width of a full tile, adjust the center point and test the layout again.

(continued)

Starting at one corner of the center intersection, apply the adhesive recommended by the manufacturer and spread it with a notched trowel. Allow adhesive to set for the recommended time, usually 30 minutes at 70°F and 50% relative humidity.

Lay the first tile at the intersection of your layout lines. Gently twist it into place and press down to work out any trapped air—but don't try to stretch or compress it. Check the edges to be sure the tile is square to the guidelines.

Lay the first quadrant. Working in one direction at a time, continue to lay tiles in the adhesive. Stop every 30 minutes and roll the tiles with a weighted floor roller to squeeze out any trapped air and maximize contact between the tile and the adhesive.

Continue laying individual tiles, checking them for square and rolling them at regular intervals. If you get adhesive on the top surface, clean it off quickly with diluted mineral spirits.

At door jambs or other obstacles, place a tile face up in place. Lean it against the obstacle and mark the point where they meet. Move the tile to find the other cut line, and mark that as well. Flip the tile over, extend the two lines using a carpenter's square, and cut out the corner with a utility knife.

To fit tile around an object, such as a pipe or drain, cut a tile-sized piece of paper. Work the paper into the space, cutting as needed until it fits around the object. Then lay the paper on a tile and use it as a cutting guide.

Work from the center outward in each quadrant. As you complete each row, check to see that all edges are straight. Hand-roll all seams after you finish each row. If there are gaps in the seams, hold them together temporarily with painter's tape and then place weight on top.

Install any trim pieces, such as baseboards, shoe base, escutcheons, and thresholds.

Ceramic, Stone & Glass Tile

Hard flooring tiles include products made from a wide variety of materials, including molded clay, ceramics, quarried stone, and glass. Although there are obviously significant differences between tile products, they are all installed using cement-based mortar or epoxy as an adhesive and grout to fill the gaps between tiles.

To ensure a long-lasting hard tile floor, you'll need a smooth, stable, structurally sound and level subfloor (see page 58). In addition, the underlayment must be solid. Cementboard, or the thinner fiber-cementboard, is the best underlayment for tile floors in kitchens and bathrooms, since it has excellent stability and is unaffected by moisture. Cementboard is manufactured exclusively for ceramic tile installation and will work well under any other type of tile.

In rooms where moisture is not a factor, exterior-grade plywood is an adequate underlayment that is less expensive than cementboard. Another option is isolation membrane, which is used to protect ceramic, stone, and glass tile from movements in the subfloor—specifically, cracked concrete. Isolation membrane can be used just to cover individual cracks, or it can be used over an entire floor.

Different types of tiles feature different coatings and sealants. You'll need to take steps to protect the surface of porous tiles that are unglazed or left in their natural state, and others, such as marble, that need regular maintenance to look their best. Seal grout lines as well to prevent them from becoming stained by dirt.

If you want to install trim tiles, consider their placement as you plan the layout. Some types of base trim tile are set on the floor, with the finished edge flush with the field tile. Other types are installed above the field tile, after the field tile has been laid and grouted.

Laying a hard tile floor is a great project for do-it-yourselfers because it is easy to take the work at your own speed and the results are very satisfying.

Tools & Materials

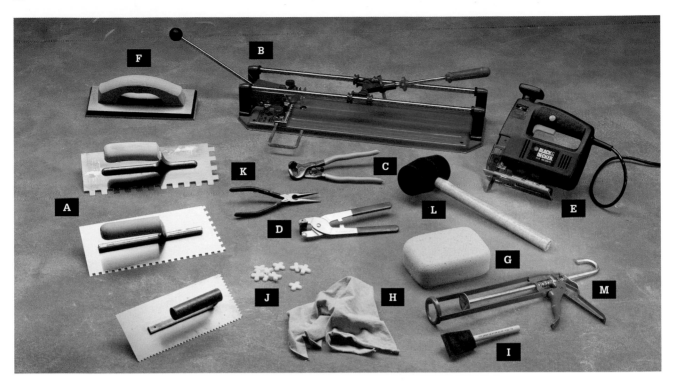

Tile tools include adhesive-spreading tools, cutting tools, and grouting tools. Notched trowels (A) for spreading mortar come with notches of varying sizes and shapes. The size of the notch should be proportional to the size of the tile being installed. Cutting tools include a tile cutter (B), tile nippers (C), hand-held tile cutter (D), and jigsaw with carbide blade (E). Grouting tools include a grout float (F), grout sponge (G), buff rag (H), and foam brush (I) for applying grout sealer. Other tile tools include spacers (J), available in different sizes to create grout joints of varying widths; needlenose pliers (K), for removing spacers; rubber mallet (L), for setting tiles into mortar; and caulk gun (M).

Tile materials include adhesives, grouts, and sealers. Thin-set mortar (A), the most common floor-tile adhesive, is often strengthened with latex mortar additive (B). Grout additive (C) can be added to floor grout (D) to make it more resilient and durable. Grout fills the spaces between tiles and is available in pre-tinted colors to match your tile. Silicone caulk (E) should be used in place of grout where tile meets another surface, like a bathtub. Use wall-tile adhesive (F) for installing base-trim tile. Grout sealer (G) and porous-tile sealer (H) ward off stains and make maintenance easier. (Inset) Trim and finishing materials include base-trim tiles (A), bullnose tiles (B), and doorway thresholds (C) in thicknesses ranging from ¼ to ¾" to match floor levels.

How to Make Straight Cuts

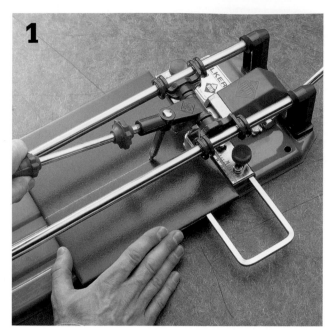

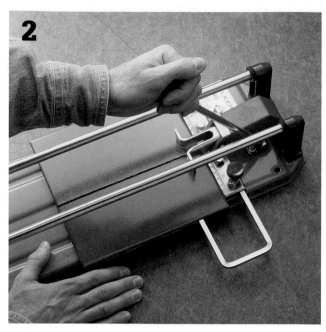

For straight cuts, mark a cutting line on the tile with a pencil, then place the tile in the cutter so the cutting wheel is directly over the line. While pressing down firmly on the wheel handle, run the wheel across the tile to score the surface. For a clean cut, score the tile only once.

Snap the tile along the scored line as directed by the tool manufacturer. Snapping the tile is usually accomplished by depressing a lever on the tile cutter

How to Make Curved Cuts

To cut curves, mark a cutting line on the tile face. Use the scoring wheel of a hand-held tile cutter to score the cut line. Make several parallel scores, no more than ¼" apart, in the waste portion of the tile.

Use tile nippers to nibble away the scored portion of the tile. To cut circular holes in the middle of a tile, score and cut the tile so it divides the hole in half, then remove waste material from each half of the circle.

Other Tile-cutting Tools

Tile saws, also called "wet saws" because they use water to cool blades and tiles, are used primarily for cutting natural-stone tiles. They're also useful for quickly cutting notches in all kinds of hard tile. Wet saws are available for rent at tile dealers and rental shops.

Use a jigsaw with a fine tungsten-carbide blade to make short cuts in tile.

A rented wet saw is a good choice for cutting square notches from floor tile.

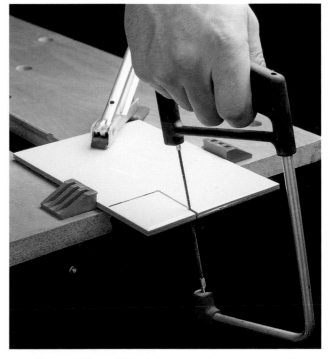

Install a carbide rod blade into a coping saw and use it to make delicate cuts in floor tile.

Installing Ceramic Floor Tile

Ceramic tile installation starts with the same steps as installing resilient tile. Snap perpendicular reference lines and dry-fit tiles to ensure the best placement.

When setting tiles, work in small sections so the mortar doesn't dry before the tiles are set.

Use spacers between tiles to ensure consistent spacing. Plan an installation sequence to avoid kneeling on set tiles. Be careful not to kneel or walk on tiles until the designated drying period is over.

Tools & Materials ▸

¼" square-notched trowel
Rubber mallet
Tile cutter
Tile nippers
Hand-held tile cutter
Needlenose pliers
Grout float
Grout sponge

Soft cloth
Thin-set mortar
Tile
Tile spacers
Grout
Latex grout additive
Wall adhesive
2 × 4 lumber

Grout sealer
Tile caulk
Sponge brush
Cementboard
Chalk line
Tape measure
Drill
Caulk gun

1¼" cementboard screws
Fiberglass-mesh wallboard tape
Utility knife or grout knife
Threshold material
Jigsaw or circular saw with a
    tungsten-carbide blade
Rounded bullnose tile
Eye protection and gloves

Floor tile can be laid in many decorative patterns, but for your first effort, it may be best to stick to a basic grid. In most cases, floor tile is combined with profiled base tile (installed after flooring).

How to Install Ceramic Floor Tile

Check that the subfloor is smooth, level, and stable.
Spread thin-set mortar on the subfloor for one sheet of
cementboard. Place the cementboard on the mortar, keeping a
¼" gap along the walls.

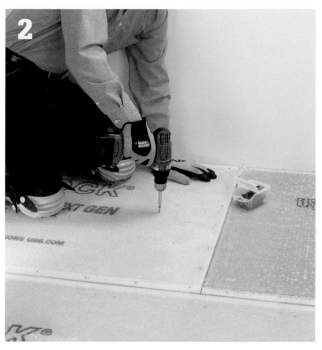

Fasten cementboard in place with 1¼" cementboard
screws. Place fiberglass-mesh wallboard tape over the seams.
Cover the remainder of the floor, following the steps on
page 66.

Draw reference lines and establish the tile layout (see
page 127). Mix a batch of thin-set mortar, then spread the
mortar evenly against both reference lines of one quadrant,
using a ¼" square-notched trowel. Use the notched edge of
the trowel to create furrows in the mortar bed.

Set the first tile in the corner of the quadrant where the
reference lines intersect. When setting tiles that are 8" square
or larger, twist each tile slightly as you set it into position.

(continued)

Using a soft rubber mallet, gently tap the central area of each tile a few times to set it evenly into the mortar.

Variation: For large tiles or uneven stone, use a larger trowel with notches that are at least ½" deep.

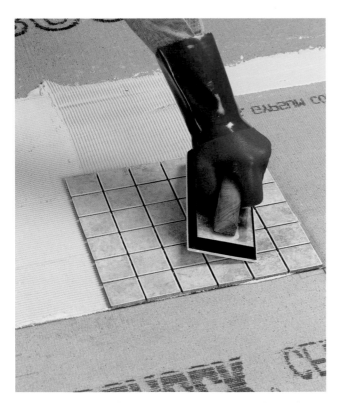

Variation: For mosaic sheets, use a ³⁄₁₆" V-notched trowel to spread the mortar and a grout float to press the sheets into the mortar. Apply pressure gently to avoid creating an uneven surface.

To ensure consistent spacing between tiles, place plastic tile spacers at the corners of the set tile. With mosaic sheets, use spacers equal to the gaps between tiles.

7

Position and set adjacent tiles into the mortar along the reference lines. Make sure the tiles fit neatly against the spacers.

8

To make sure the tiles are level with one another, place a straight piece of 2 × 4 across several tiles, then tap the board with a mallet.

9

Lay tile in the remaining area covered with mortar. Repeat steps 2 to 8, continuing to work in small sections, until you reach walls or fixtures.

10

Measure and mark tiles to fit against walls and into corners. Cut the tiles to fit. Apply thin-set mortar directly to the back of the cut tiles, instead of the floor, using the notched edge of the trowel to furrow the mortar.

(continued)

Set the cut pieces of tile into position. Press down on the tile until each piece is level with adjacent tiles.

Measure, cut, and install tiles that require notches or curves to fit around obstacles, such as exposed pipes or toilet drains.

Carefully remove the spacers with needlenose pliers before the mortar hardens.

Apply mortar and set tiles in the remaining quadrants, completing one quadrant before starting the next. Inspect all tile joints and use a utility knife or grout knife to remove any high spots of mortar that could show through the grout.

Install threshold material in doorways. If the threshold is too long for the doorway, cut it to fit with a jigsaw or circular saw and a tungsten-carbide blade. Set the threshold in thin-set mortar so the top is even with the tile. Keep the same space between the threshold as between tiles. Let the mortar set for at least 24 hours.

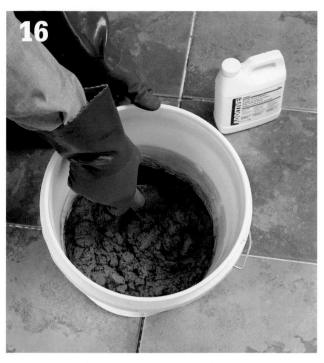

Prepare a small batch of floor grout to fill the tile joints. When mixing grout for porous tile, such as quarry or natural stone, use an additive with a release agent to prevent grout from bonding to the tile surfaces.

Starting in a corner, pour the grout over the tile. Use a rubber grout float to spread the grout outward from the corner, pressing firmly on the float to completely fill the joints. For best results, tilt the float at a 60° angle to the floor and use a figure eight motion.

Use the grout float to remove excess grout from the surface of the tile. Wipe diagonally across the joints, holding the float in a near-vertical position. Continue applying grout and wiping off excess until about 25 square feet of the floor has been grouted.

(continued)

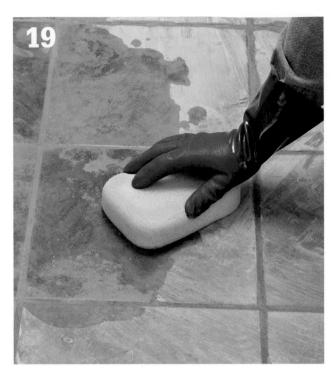

19

Wipe a damp grout sponge diagonally over about 2 square feet of the floor at a time. Rinse the sponge in cool water between wipes. Wipe each area only once since repeated wiping can pull grout back out of joints. Repeat steps 15 to 18 to apply grout to the rest of the floor.

20

Allow the grout to dry for about 4 hours, then use a soft cloth to buff the tile surface and remove any remaining grout film.

21

Apply grout sealer to the grout lines, using a small sponge brush or sash brush. Avoid brushing sealer on to the tile surfaces. Wipe up any excess sealer immediately.

Option: Use a tile sealer to seal porous tile, such as quarry tile or unglazed tile. Following the manufacturer's instructions, roll a thin coat of sealer over the tile and grout joints using a paint roller and extension handle.

How to Install Bullnose Base Trim

Dry-fit the tiles to determine the best spacing. Grout lines in base tile do not always align with grout lines in the floor tile. Use rounded bullnose tiles at outside corners, and mark tiles for cutting as needed.

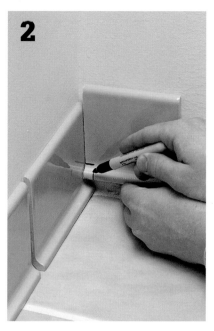

Leaving a ⅛" expansion gap between tiles at corners, mark any contour cuts necessary to allow the coved edges to fit together. Use a jigsaw with a tungsten-carbide blade to make curved cuts.

Begin installing base-trim tiles at an inside corner. Use a notched trowel to apply wall adhesive to the back of the tile. Place ⅛" spacers on the floor under each tile to create an expansion joint.

Press the tile onto the wall. Continue setting tiles, using spacers to maintain ⅛" gaps between the tiles and ⅛" expansion joints between the tiles and floor.

Use a double-bullnose tile on one side of outside corners to cover the edge of the adjoining tile.

After the adhesive dries, grout the vertical joints between tiles and apply grout along the tops of the tiles to make a continuous grout line. Once the grout hardens, fill the expansion joint between the tiles and floor with caulk.

Mosaic Tile

Mosaic tile is an excellent choice for smaller areas. It requires the same preparation and handling as larger tiles, with a few differences. Sheets of mosaic tile are held together by a fabric-mesh base. This makes them more difficult to hold, place, and move. They may not be square with your guidelines when you first lay them down. And mosaic tiles will require many more temporary spacers and much more grout.

A few cautions: variations in color and texture are just as likely with mosaic tile as with individual tiles, so buy all your tile from the same lot and batch. Different types of tiles will require different types of mortar and mastic. Finally, if the finished project will be exposed to the elements, make sure you have adhesive and grout suitable for outdoor use.

Tools & Materials ▸

Carpenter's square
Chalk line
Cleaning supplies
Coarse sponge
Grout sealer
Marking pen
   or pencil
Measuring tape
Notched trowel

Recommended
   adhesive
Rubber mallet
Sanded grout
Scrap lumber
Tile nippers
Tile spacers
Mosaic tile sheets
Grout float

Mosaic tiles come in sheets (usually 12 × 12") and can be made from ceramic, porcelain, glass or any number of designer materials. Normally installed for their appearance, mosaics are relatively high maintenance and prone to cracks because of all the grout lines.

How to Install Mosaic Tile

Clean and prepare the area as you would for individual tiles, with reference lines beginning in the center. Beginning at the center intersection, apply the recommended adhesive to one quadrant. Spread it outward evenly with a notched trowel. Lay down only as much adhesive as you can cover in 10 to 15 minutes.

Select a sheet of mosaic tile. Place several plastic spacers within the grid so that the sheet remains square. Pick up the sheet of tiles by diagonally opposite corners. This will help you hold the edges up so that you don't trap empty space in the middle of the sheet.

3

Gently press one corner into place on the adhesive. Slowly lower the opposite corner, making sure the sides remain square with your reference lines. Massage the sheet into the adhesive, being careful not to press too hard or twist the sheet out of position. Insert a few spacers in the outside edges of the sheet you have just placed. This will help keep the grout lines consistent.

4

When you have placed two or three sheets, lay a scrap piece of flat lumber across the tops and tap the wood with a rubber mallet to set the fabric mesh in the adhesive, and to force out any trapped air. *Note: Staple scrap carpet material to the lumber to protect the tile surface.*

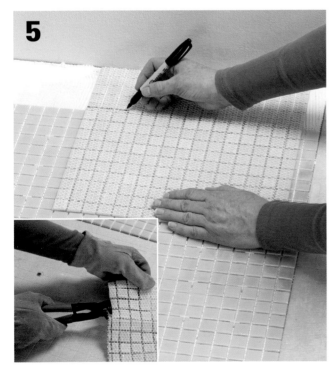

5

At the outer edges of your work area, you will probably need to trim one or more rows from the last sheet. If the space left at the edge is more than the width of a regular grout line, use tile nippers to trim the last row that will fit. Save these leftover tiles for repairs.

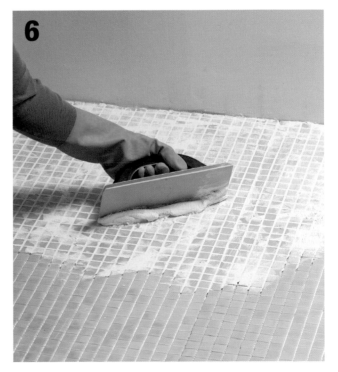

6

After the adhesive has cured, usually 24 to 48 hours, apply grout as you would for individual tiles. With many more spaces, mosaic tiles will require more grout. Follow the manufacturer's instructions for spreading and floating the grout. Clean up using the instructions for individual tiles (see page 150).

Glass Tiles ▶

Largely lost in the bounty of ceramic and stone choices, glass tile deserves serious consideration for the dynamic impact it can make in a kitchen or bathroom. Boasting elegant, jewel-like colors, this type of tile can create a truly unique and stunning floor.

The secret of glass tile's attraction is the color. Pigment is added during the actual production of the glass, meaning that the color is inherent in the material—it won't fade, wear off or otherwise change. Of course, as durable as the color is, the glass surface itself can be chipped. Still, the thickness of the tiles themselves ensures that they won't crack under normal wear.

Installing glass tiles is just slightly more challenging than laying a floor of stone or ceramic tile. The goal is to create a bright white background against which the color

of the tile will pop. To this end, some manufacturers back their glass with a white base. All specify the use of a white crack suppression membrane under the tile and bright white thinset mortar to bed the tiles. Glass tiles are cut on a wet saw just like many stone tiles are, but the saw must be equipped with a diamond blade made for cutting glass. The finished floor is grouted in the same way that a ceramic tile floor would be.

The white subsurface and backing give glass tile floors an almost luminous quality, as if the floor were lit from within. It's a clean, sophisticated, modern look that calls attention to itself. This type of floor is therefore best suited to simple, uncluttered, and largely monochromatic color schemes that won't compete with the bright hues of the floor. But used in the right space, glass floor tiles offer a design element that is a feast for the eyes.

Relatively plain ceramic floor tiles take on new life and vivaciousness when framed with a border of glass tiles. Here, the glass tile border also makes a stunning transition from the ceramic tile floor to a carpeted area.

Hexagonal glass mosaic tiles hearken back the Art Deco era of the early to mid Twentieth Century, but the texture, the luminescence and the contemporary wasabi color clearly identify this as a modern floor. The floor pairs beautifully with the reproduction vitreous china lavatory with its round steel legs. Accent tiles in a floral display create a highlight near the door.

The glass wall tile is definitely the star of this bathroom, but the effect succeeds largely because of the rustic slate tile floor. Not infrequently, mosaic glass tile is carried through to the floor as well. This can be effective, but if it is not handled with some design skill it can quickly become dizzying.

Glass tiles come in unlimited color options. Choosing a few you like and blending them together adds a lot of visual interest to the floor and creates opportunities to pull out color from neighboring surfaces, fixtures and decorative elements. Because glass tile is installed on a white substrate, even very muted colors read instantly; this allows you to mix and match with much less risk than if the colors were bolder.

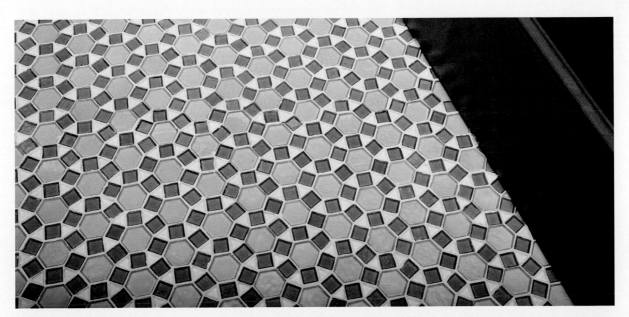

Custom glass tile designs make a bold statement. This sophisticated arrangement of hexagons, squares and triangles is created in mosaic sheets at the tile manufacturing facility. Creating your own unique design and color scheme is great fun, but it does add considerably to the cost.

Combination Tile

This hybrid product combines the classic, refined look of ceramic tile with the easy installation of resilient flooring. Made to resemble a range of hard materials, from slate to quarry tile to marble, combination tiles feel warmer and more comfortable underfoot than ordinary ceramic tile.

Designs vary from brand to brand, but most major manufacturers of resilient tile now offer combination products as well. You can install them like regular resilient tile, with each tile placed tightly against the next, or you can leave spaces between the squares and add grout to replicate the look and feel of regular ceramic tile.

With or without grout, combination tile, also known as compound resilient tile, is easy to maintain.

Some manufacturers offer generous warranties, promising that the tiles will not fade, stain, crack, or show wear for many years. This confidence translates to peace of mind for you.

Tools & Materials ▸

Tape measure
Chalk line
1/16" notched trowel
Combination tile
Flooring adhesive
Weighted roller

Joint sealer
Cleaning supplies
Coping saw (or cutting tool recommended by manufacturer)
Grout (optional)

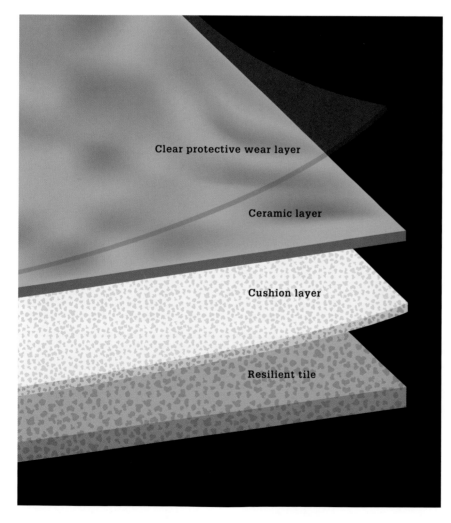

Clear protective wear layer

Ceramic layer

Cushion layer

Resilient tile

In kitchens and bathrooms, floor coverings need to withstand heavy traffic, frequent cleaning, and lots of moisture. Ceramic tile meets these needs, but it can be difficult to install, feels cold underfoot, and is not forgiving with dropped dishes. Vinyl, in sheets or tiles, makes a softer, warmer surface that is inexpensive and relatively easy to install. But vinyl is vulnerable to scrapes and gouges and doesn't last as long as ceramic tile. In recent years, manufacturers have found ways of using the best properties of both materials in combination tiles. These vinyl tiles are covered with a thin layer of ceramic composite. They can be installed like regular vinyl tiles, with their edges pushed together, or with spaces left for grout.

Combination tile cultivates the beauty and durability of stone or ceramic tile and adds the comfort and warmth of vinyl flooring. The resulting material is truly the best of both worlds.

How to Install Combination Tile

Compound resilient tiles can be installed on a variety of surfaces. Check the manufacturer's instructions to make sure your underlayment is recommended. It should be clean, dry, and free of dust, dirt, grease, and wax. Sweep, vacuum, and damp-mop the surface before you begin.

Measure the outside edges of the room. Find the middle point on opposite walls and snap chalk lines between them. The intersection of the lines should be in the middle of the room.

Starting at the central intersection, dry-lay a row of tiles to one wall. If the last tile will be less than ¼ the width of a full tile, you may want to move the center point.

Re-mark your layout lines to match your adjusted center point from step 3. Check the central intersecting lines for square using the 3-4-5 method.

Avoid positioning tile joints directly over underlayment joints or seams in existing flooring. If this happens, reposition the chalk lines to offset joints by at least 3" or half the width of one tile. Repeat the dry-laying test, adjusting the lines as needed, until you have a definite starting point.

Apply the recommended adhesive to one quadrant of the center intersection with a notched trowel. Let adhesive set for the time specified by the manufacturer and then lay tiles along the layout lines. Use only as much adhesive as you can cover during the working time allowed. Continue to work from the center outward in each quadrant.

To work around obstacles, place the tile up against the obstacle and mark cut lines. Follow manufacturer instructions for cutting tile.

Within an hour after the tiles are set, roll the floor with a weighted roller. Work in both directions, taking care not to push any tiles out of place. Re-roll the floor before grouting the tiles or applying a joint sealer.

Porcelain Snap-lock Tile

Porcelain snap-lock tile flooring is a relatively new innovation that combines the easy installation of laminate floors with the durability and feel of ceramic tile. Each square porcelain tile is placed on a plastic tray with interlocking tabs all around on top of a rubberized non-skid base. The construction allows the tiles to be assembled into a floating floor that requires no adhesive and ensures the feel underfoot is remarkably similar to a conventional tile floor.

The floating floor installation makes this type of tile floor much quicker to lay, less expensive, and it can be replaced with far less hassle than a floor installed in a bed of adhesive. The floor can also be installed over any clean and stable existing surface as long as variations in the floor surface don't exceed ¼-inch over a 10-foot span. You can also choose from 12-inch or four-inch square tiles. Once sealed with the flexible grout supplied by the manufacturer, the floor is as resistant to moisture as any tile floor.

The one drawback to the snap-lock porcelain tile currently on the market is the palette of colors, which is currently limited to a family of earth-tone beiges and browns. However, these colors do blend with a wide range of décor schemes. The mottled satin finish is also easy to clean and doesn't show dirt between cleanings. And, as the technology catches on, more and more colors will likely become available.

Tools & Materials ▸

Snap-lock tiles (See Resources, page 266)	Utility knife
	Mallet
Carpenter's square	Flexible grout
Rubber tapping block	Grout float
Rubber coated pull bar	Sponge
Eye and ear protection	Circular saw
Trowel	Tape measure
Wet saw	Gloves
Angle grinder	

The look and feel of traditional ceramic tile is achieved with these snap-together tiles made up of a porcelain ceramic surface over a substrate that has interlocking tabs (inset). Flexible grout is the key to this system's workability.

How to Install a Snap-Lock Tile Floor

Check the door swing for all doors in the room to make sure they will clear the new tile floor. If the door won't clear, or if the gap between the door and the floor is less than ¼", remove and shorten the door. Flush-cut the door casings to allow for tile clearance, and remove shoe molding and all appliances and fixtures that block access to the floor.

Check that walls are square using a carpenter's square or the 3-4-5 measurement method. If walls are out of square, decide how you will adjust rows to compensate. Also measure floor width and decide if you want to place the first row in the center of the floor or begin at a wall.

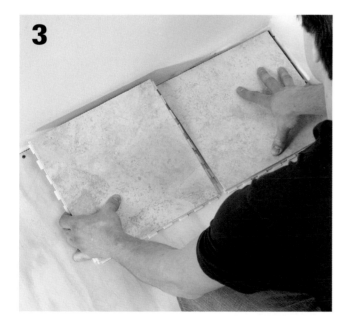

Lay the first two tiles after removing the lock tabs on the wall-facing side or sides using a sharp utility knife. Start placing tiles in the corner and leave a ¼" expansion gap between the tiles and the walls. Although the locking tabs project out ¼" from the tiles and thus would function as ¼" spacers, the fact that they are integral parts of the tiles makes this gap ineffective as an expansion gap. Use traditional removable spacers. Attach each new tile by aligning the tiles, connecting at the corner and then pressing together until the tiles lock.

Use a rubber tapping block if you have difficulty engaging the locking tabs by simply pressing them together. Align the tiles, then hold the block against the side of the tile—not the plastic tray or grid. Gently tap the block until the tiles lock together.

(continued)

5

Continue to lay tiles, paying careful attention to layout patterns and directional veining in the tile surfaces. If you make a mistake and need to remove and adjust a tile, you can disconnect the joints with a rubber coated pull bar or any other prying tool with a protective surface coating. Place the tool edge between the two tiles and gently pry them apart.

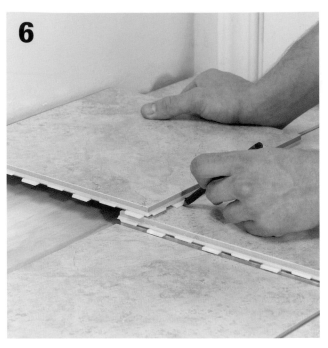

6

Mark tiles to fit around obstacles or for the final row by laying one tile on top and aligning with the previous row. Then lay a tile on top of that one, and align within ¼" of the wall or obstacle. Mark a cutline on the middle tile using the space between the tabs of the top tile as guidance.

7

Cut tiles using a wet saw with a blade meant for cutting ceramic and porcelain tiles. Cut on waste side of marked line, and change water in basin frequently to ensure clean cuts. Porcelain takes a long time to cut. Be patient and do not force the tile into the saw blade.

Cutting Curves ▶

To cut curves and other irregular shapes, use an angle grinder that's fitted with a diamond-tipped cutting wheel. Cut all the way through the tile, including the plastic base layer. This will take several passes. *Note: The tiles seen here have very aggressive anti-skid ribs on the bottom and do not require securing to the worksurface as a typical workpiece would.*

8

Set final tiles into position and then pull them back into the preceding rows using a rubberized pull bar. When the floor is completed, open the pail of flexible grout and mix thoroughly with a trowel according to the manufacturer's instructions.

9

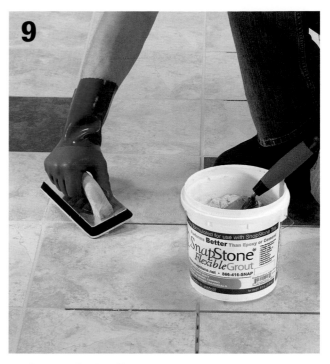

Apply grout in the tile gaps with a firm rubber grout float. Spread grout diagonally to the tile joints, working the grout firmly into the joints. Remove excess grout from the tiles with the edge of the float and touch up voids or low areas in the grout joints.

10

Clean off excess grout. Fill a 5 gal. bucket with clean water and use a sponge to clean the surfaces of the tiles. Wipe off grout residue and use sponge to smooth grout lines. *Important: Rinse the sponge thoroughly with clean water after each pass.*

Replacing a Damaged Tile ▸

To replace a porcelain snap-lock tile that has been cracked or damaged, remove the grout all around the tile. Use a grout cutter or simply chip out the grout with an awl or fine chisel. In either case, be careful not to chip the surrounding tiles. Then cut the downward-facing tabs on three sides of the tile with a utility knife. Pry up the broken tile and pull away from the uncut side. Remove downward tabs on three sides of the new tile and lay a bed of general construction adhesive under the new tile. Slide the new tile into place and lock the uncut side to the adjacent tile. Let adhesive dry and grout with flexible grout.

Interlocking Utility Tile

Interlocking floor tiles are a quick, DIY-friendly solution that can give your garage or basement floor a custom checkerboard look. These 1 × 1-foot tiles are molded in a range of colors and are made of recycled PVC or other composites. There are several surface pattern styles to choose from, depending on the manufacturer. Some types are ventilated to promote drying, which makes them a good option for installing over damp concrete. The tiles will resist gasoline, oil, and most other solvents, so they're well suited for garage or workshop applications.

Interlocking tiles create a floating floor system. The four edges have locking tabs that clip together like a jigsaw puzzle. Once installed, the tile grid holds itself in place, so there's no need to fasten or glue the tiles permanently to the concrete subfloor. You can cut them with standard woodworking saws and tap them together with a mallet. Most tile brands offer beveled transition pieces as well.

The process for installing locking floor tiles is quite similar to laying permanent floor tile. Clean the floor thoroughly, then measure it and snap chalk lines to determine the exact center. Start by laying a row of tiles along the intersecting chalk line. Adjust the row as needed to allow for full tiles along the edges. It's fine to have partial tiles along the back wall. Now, build out the tile grid left and right of the center row to fill in the rest of the floor. Measure and cut partial tiles as needed to fit against the side and back walls. Finish by adding beveled transition pieces if necessary, and cover the edges of the floor at the walls with sanitary base or other base moldings. With a helper, you should be able to complete this project in an afternoon.

Tools & Materials ▸

Push broom or leaf blower	Rubber mallet
Tape measure	Jigsaw or circular saw
Chalk line	Grease pencil
Stiff-bristle brush	Surface sealer
Cleaning detergent	Floor tiles
Backer board	Clamps
Plastic bucket	Eye and ear
Straightedge guide	protection
	Base molding

Interlocking floor tiles snap together for a virtually foolproof installation, and you'll have all the conveniences that a floating floor can offer.

How to Install Interlocking Floor Tiles

1

Clean the floor by sweeping, vacuuming, or blowing off any debris with a leaf blower.

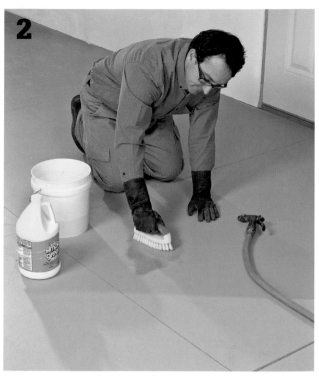

2

Remove any oily stains by scrubbing with detergent and a stiff-bristle brush.

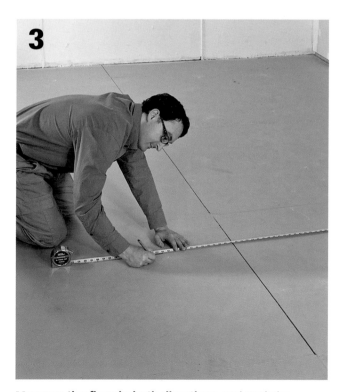

3

Measure the floor in both directions, and mark the locations of the centerlines.

4

Snap chalk lines to connect the center points in both directions, forming a point of intersection in the middle of the garage and dividing the floor into four quadrants.

(continued)

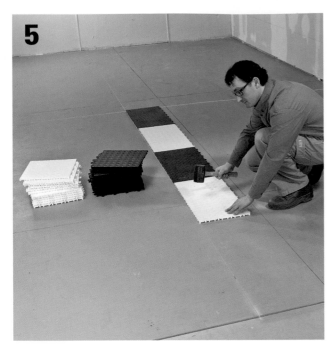

Lay tiles along one leg of the layout reference line, stopping just short of the wall. Snap the tiles together as you work. Use a rubber mallet to gently tap and set the tiles, if necessary.

Adjust the position of the first row of tiles so the last tile will fit just short of the wall or overhead door opening without cutting. It is best to have the cut tiles against the far wall. If you plan to install a beveled transition strip (some, but not all, manufacturers carry them), be sure to allow room for it when repositioning the row. Snap new chalk lines parallel to the originals to accommodate your new layout.

Add tiles along the adjusted reference lines to establish the layout. If you find that one row of tiles will need to terminate with tiles that are cut to a couple of inches or less, adjust the layout side to side so the cut tiles will be evenly balanced at both ends of the line. Fill in the tiles in the field area of all quadrants.

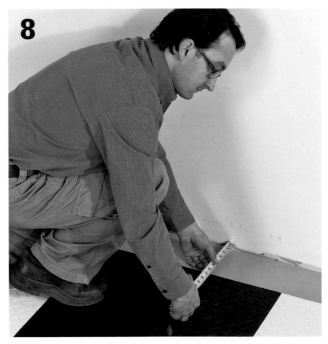

Measure the gaps at the ends of the rows requiring cut tiles and subtract ¼" for expansion.

9

Cut the tiles that need cutting with a jigsaw. Be sure to place a backer board underneath the tile. Use a straightedge guide for a clean cut.

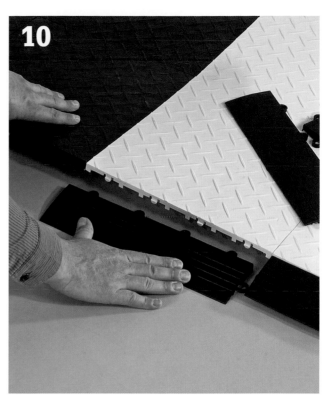

10

Install transition strips at doorways. Not all brands of interlocking tiles have transition strips available.

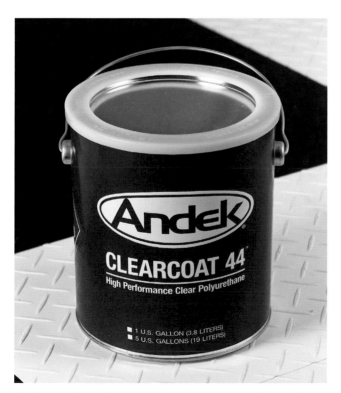

Option: Seal the tiles to protect against damage by applying a surface sealer. (Check with the tile manufacturer for its recommendations.)

11

Add base trim. Conceal the expansion gaps around the perimeter of the installation with molding, such as vinyl-cove base molding.

Bonded Rubber Roll Flooring

Once a mark of restaurants and retailers, sheet rubber flooring has become an option for homeowners as well. It's resilient, durable, and stable, holding up well under the heaviest and most demanding use. Better still, it's comfortable to walk on and easy to maintain.

The durability and resilience of rubber provide benefits in two ways. First, the flooring takes just about any kind of use without showing damage. Second, it absorbs shock in proportion to its thickness. Heavier rubber floors help prevent fatigue, making them comfortable for standing, walking, and even strenuous exercise.

Many new flooring products are made from recycled rubber, which saves landfill space and reduces the consumption of new raw materials. This is one place a petroleum-based product is environmentally friendly.

To install rubber sheet flooring on top of wood, use only exterior-grade plywood, one side sanded. Do not use lauan plywood, particleboard, chipboard, or hardboard underlayment. Make sure the surface is level, smooth, and securely fastened to the subfloor.

Tools & Materials ▸

Adhesive	Painter's tape
Chalk line	Straightedge
Cleaning supplies	Weighted floor roller
Craft/utility knife	Hand roller
Measuring tape	Base moldings
Mineral spirits	Eye protection
Notched trowel	and gloves

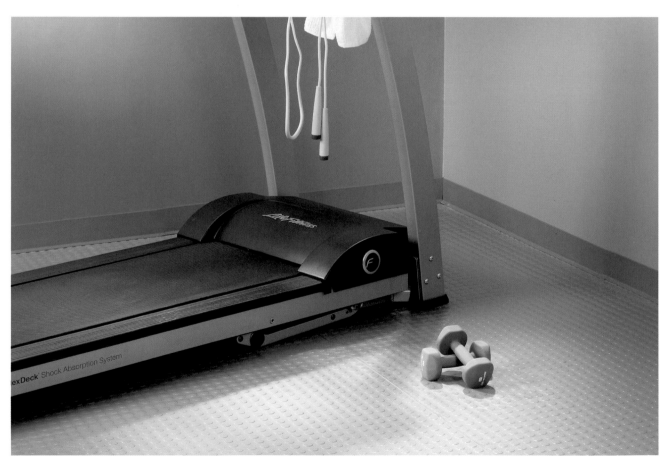

Rubber roll flooring can withstand rigorous use without showing damage and is shock-absorbent, making it a great solution for workshops or exercise rooms.

How to Install Rubber Roll Flooring

Mark the first strip of rubber roll flooring for cutting to length. Start on the longest wall, and mark the cutting line so the strip will be a couple of inches too long. Use a straightedge guide to mark the cutting lines, and then cut with a sharp utility knife (be sure to put a backer board under the material before cutting it).

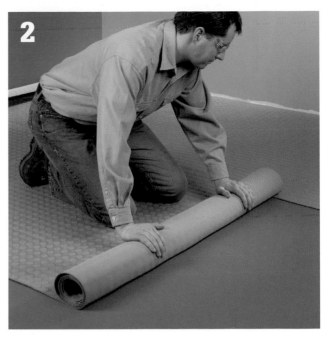

Set the first strip against the long wall so the overage in length is equal at each end. Cut the next strip to length and then butt it up against the first strip. Adjust the second strip so it overlaps the first strip by 1 to 1½", making sure the strips remain parallel. Lay out all of the strips in the room in this manner.

Cut the strips to create perfectly matched seams. With a backer board underneath the seam, center a straightedge on the top strip and carefully cut through both strips in the overlap area. Change utility knife blades frequently, and don't try to make the cut in one pass unless your flooring is very thin.

Remove the waste material from the seam area and test the fit of the strips. Because they were cut together, they should align perfectly. Make sure you don't adjust the position of one of the strips or the seams may not align properly.

(continued)

Fold back half of the first strip so half of the flooring subbase is exposed. Again, take care not to shift the position of the flooring strip.

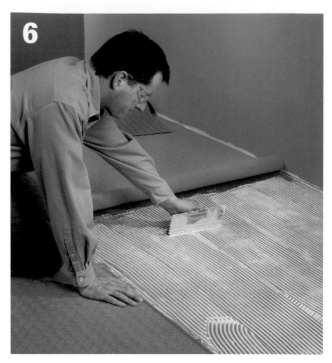

Apply the adhesive recommended by the flooring manufacturer to the exposed floor, using a notched trowel. Avoid getting adhesive on the surface of the flooring, and make sure the adhesive is applied all the way up to the walls and just past the seam area.

Lower the roll slowly onto the adhesive, making sure not to allow any air to become trapped underneath. Never leave adhesive ridges or puddles; they will become visible on the surface.

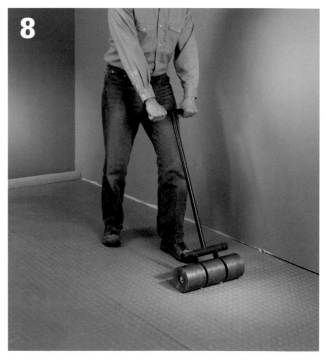

Roll the floor immediately with a 100 lb. roller to squeeze out any trapped air and maximize contact between the roll and the adhesive. With each pass of the roller, overlap the previous pass by half. Roll the width first, then the length, and roll again after 30 minutes.

Fold back the second half of the first roll, and the first half of the second roll. Apply and spread the adhesive as before. Spread the adhesive at a 90° angle to the seams. This will reduce the chance of having adhesive squeeze up through the seams. Continue installing strips in this manner.

Clean up adhesive squeezeout or spills immediately using a rag and mineral spirits. At seams, take care not to allow mineral spirits to get underneath the flooring, as it will ruin the adhesive.

Press down on any bubbles or on seams that do not have a seamless appearance. If a seam resists lying flat, set a board and weights over it overnight. It is a good idea to hand-roll all seams with a J-roller, in addition to rolling the entire floor with a floor roller.

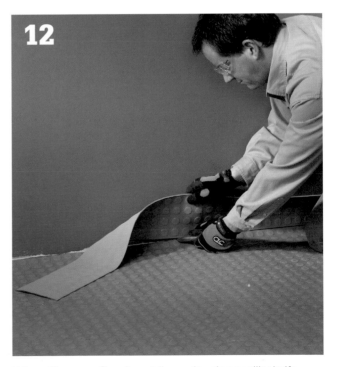

Trim off excess flooring at the ends using a utility knife. Leaving a slight gap between the flooring and the wall is fine as long as you plan to install base molding.

Seamed Rubber Roll Flooring

Heavy-duty rolled flooring is manufactured in several colors and surface textures, including rib, coin, and tread patterns. This is the soft floor covering you often see in airports, shopping malls, gyms, and other high-traffic areas. The material is impervious to most chemicals as well as road salt and water and is heavy enough to stay in place without adhesive. Patterns help to hide minor concrete blemishes and improve traction. Rolled flooring is manufactured in 7½- to 10-foot-wide rolls and in various lengths up to 60 feet.

Installing roll-out covering requires much less preparation than permanent floor coverings, and the material is thick enough to lay flat and stay in place without bonding it to the concrete. To prepare for installation, sweep and clean your floor. Use cleaning chemicals, and then rinse thoroughly to remove stubborn oil and chemical stains. Plan to install the flooring on a warm, sunny day.

Tools & Materials ▶

Stiff-bristle push broom
Double-sided carpet tape
Roll-out floor covering

Tape measure
Straightedge
Utility knife

Roll-out flooring is a durable floating-floor solution that requires no special adhesives to install. In fact, you can lift up and pull the sheets outside for easy cleaning. It's an excellent option for concealing aged, stained, or damp concrete slabs.

How to Install Seamed Roll Flooring

1

2

Unroll the flooring material, preferably in a clean driveway on a sunny day. Let the material rest for a few hours to flatten.

Lay the material on the floor in rough position and use a push broom to sweep out any air bubbles.

3

4

Trim the material to fit around door openings and any obstructions using a sharp utility knife. For larger spaces, roll out additional rolls of floor covering as needed.

Tape seams between rolls by curling the edge over and applying double-sided carpet tape to one roll. Lay the edges back down so the edge of the other roll is pressed into the tape.

Resilient Sheet Vinyl

Preparing a perfect underlayment is the most important phase of resilient sheet vinyl installation (see page 64). Cutting the material to fit the contours of the room is a close second.

The best way to ensure accurate cuts is to make a cutting template. Some manufacturers offer template kits, or you can make one by following the instructions on page 177. Be sure to use the recommended adhesive for the sheet vinyl you are installing. Many manufacturers require that you use the glue they provide for installation.

Use extreme care when handling the sheet vinyl, especially felt-backed products, to avoid creasing and tearing.

Tools & Materials ▸

Linoleum knife	Heat gun
Framing square	Straightedge
Compass	Vinyl flooring
Scissors	Masking tape
Non-permanent	Heavy butcher paper
felt-tipped pen	Duct tape
Utility knife	Flooring adhesive
¼" V-notched trowel	⅜" staples
J-roller	Metal threshold bars
Stapler	Nails
Flooring roller	Wallboard knife

Sheet vinyl is a classic flooring material that is easy to install and effortless to maintain.

Tools for Installing Resilient Floors

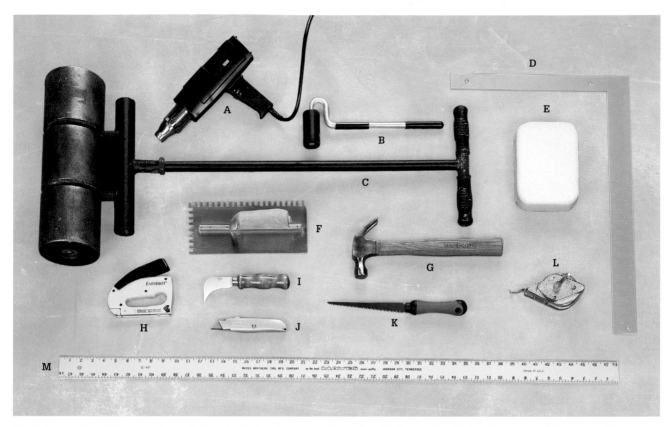

Tools for resilient flooring installation include a heat gun (A), J-roller (B), floor roller (C), framing square (D), sponge (E), notched trowel (F), hammer (G), stapler (H), linoleum knife (I), utility knife (J), wallboard saw (K), chalk line (L), straightedge (M).

Resilient Flooring Types

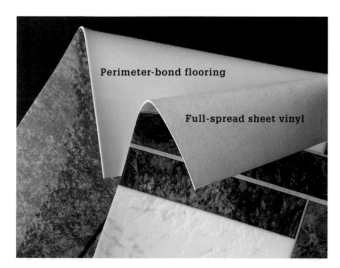

Resilient sheet vinyl comes in full-spread and perimeter-bond styles. Full-spread sheet vinyl has a felt-paper backing and is secured with adhesive that is spread over the floor before installation. Perimeter-bond flooring, identifiable by its smooth, white PVC backing, is laid directly on underlayment and is secured by a special adhesive spread along the edges and seams.

Resilient tile comes in self-adhesive and dry-back styles. Self-adhesive tile has a pre-applied adhesive protected by wax paper backing that is peeled off as the tiles are installed. Dry-back tile is secured with adhesive spread onto the underlayment before installation. Self-adhesive tile is easier to install than dry-back tile, but the bond is less reliable. Don't use additional adhesives with self-adhesive tile.

Sweep and vacuum the underlayment thoroughly before installing resilient flooring to ensure a smooth, flawless finish (left). Small pieces of debris can create noticeable bumps in the flooring (right).

Handle resilient sheet vinyl carefully to avoid creasing or tearing (right). Working with a helper can help prevent costly mistakes (left). Make sure the sheet vinyl is at room temperature before you handle it.

How to Make a Cutting Template

Place sheets of heavy butcher paper or brown wrapping paper along the walls, leaving a ⅛" expansion gap. Cut triangular holes in the paper with a utility knife. Fasten the template to the floor by placing masking tape over the holes.

Follow the outline of the room, working with one sheet of paper at a time. Overlap the edges of adjoining sheets by about 2" and tape the sheets together.

To fit the template around pipes, tape sheets of paper on either side. Measure the distance from the wall to the center of the pipe, then subtract ⅛".

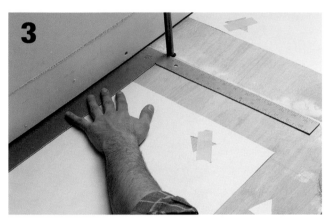

Transfer the measurement to a separate piece of paper. Use a compass to draw the pipe diameter on the paper, then cut out the hole with scissors or a utility knife. Cut a slit from the edge of the paper to the hole.

Fit the hole cutout around the pipe. Tape the hole template to the adjoining sheets.

When completed, roll or loosely fold the paper template for carrying.

How to Install Perimeter-bond Sheet Vinyl

Unroll the flooring on any large, flat, clean surface. To prevent wrinkles, sheet vinyl comes from the manufacturer rolled with the pattern-side out. Unroll the sheet and turn it pattern-side up for marking.

For two-piece installations, overlap the edges of the sheets by at least 2". Plan to have the seams fall along the pattern lines or simulated grout joints. Align the sheets so the pattern matches, then tape the sheets together with duct tape.

Make a paper template (see page 177) and position it. Trace the outline of the template onto the flooring using a non-permanent felt-tipped pen.

Remove the template. Cut the sheet vinyl with a sharp linoleum knife or a utility knife with a new blade. Use a straightedge as a guide for making longer cuts.

Cut holes for pipes and other permanent obstructions. Cut a slit from each hole to the nearest edge of the flooring. Whenever possible, make slits along pattern lines.

Roll up the flooring loosely and transfer it to the installation area. Do not fold the flooring. Unroll and position the sheet vinyl carefully. Slide the edges beneath undercut door casings.

Cut the seams for two-piece installations using a straightedge as a guide. Hold the straightedge tightly against the flooring, and cut along the pattern lines through both pieces of vinyl flooring.

Remove both pieces of scrap flooring. The pattern should now run continuously across the adjoining sheets of flooring.

Fold back the edges of both sheets. Apply a 3" band of multipurpose flooring adhesive to the underlayment or old flooring, using a ¼" V-notched trowel or wallboard knife.

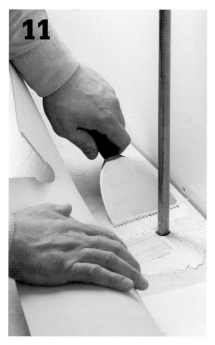

Lay the seam edges one at a time onto the adhesive. Make sure the seam is tight, pressing the gaps together with your fingers, if needed. Roll the seam edges with a J-roller or wallpaper seam roller.

Apply flooring adhesive underneath flooring cuts at pipes or posts and around the entire perimeter of the room. Roll the flooring with the roller to ensure good contact with the adhesive.

If you're applying flooring over a wood underlayment, fasten the outer edges of the sheet with ⅜" staples driven every 3". Make sure the staples will be covered by the base molding.

No-glue Sheet Vinyl

The latest in the sheet-vinyl world is a "loose-lay" (no-glue) product. It has a fiberglass backing, which makes it cushier than standard felt-backed vinyl. The fiberglass backing also makes this sheet product thicker and more dimensionally stable. Consequently, it only needs to be adhered at seams or under heavy appliances. Also, rather than using glue, you use acrylic double-sided adhesive tape.

No-glue sheet vinyl is installed in much the same way as other resilient sheet goods. Cutting the material to size is the most difficult part of the project. Fortunately, the major manufacturers have kits available to help you do it right.

This loose-lay sheet vinyl can be installed over many surfaces, including a single layer of sheet vinyl or vinyl tile, underlayment-grade plywood, concrete, or ceramic tile. Do not install over particleboard, cushioned vinyl flooring, carpet, strip wood, or plank flooring. Use embossing leveler to fill textured vinyl or ceramic grout lines, or use patching compound on plywood to create a flat, smooth surface. Do not use carpet tape for this product, as it will cause discoloration. Use standard threshold transition moldings where the sheet vinyl meets other floor surfaces.

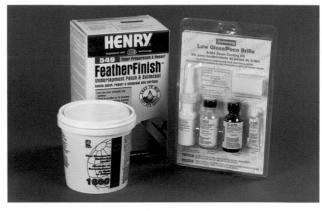

Supplies for installing no-glue sheet vinyl include a floor leveler and patching compound for preparing the floor, reinforced double-sided tape, and a seaming kit for larger installations.

Thicker than standard sheet vinyl flooring, no-glue sheet vinyl is designed to remain flat and stay put without the use of glues or other adhesives.

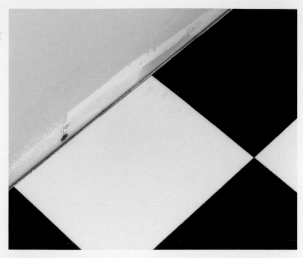

Leave gaps. To allow for the normal movement and expansion of the floor and wall surfaces, the flooring must be cut ³⁄₁₆ to ¼" away from all vertical surfaces such as walls, cabinets, or pipes. Use a jamb saw to undercut door trim—this will allow for expansion. Make sure vinyl is not contacting the wall surface behind the door trim. Check the fit of the no-glue flooring and then carefully remove the flooring.

Place acrylic double-face tape in areas that will be under heavy appliances such as stoves and refrigerators. Make an X with three pieces of tape—one long piece and two short pieces—so that the tape does not overlap. Place acrylic double-face tape at doorways and under seam lines. Leave the paper covering in place and press the tape down so it adheres well to the subfloor.

Center the tape under the two sides at seam lines. Press one side of the vinyl into place first. Place the second vinyl sheet and press it into place. Use a seam sealer kit to seal the seams.

Drive nails into the wall surface—not through the vinyl flooring—when installing the baseboard or base shoe. Anchoring the flooring with perimeter nails may result in buckling of the vinyl surface when the floor expands or contracts. Also, do not press the molding down into the vinyl. Leave a small gap between the molding and the floor surface so the vinyl is not constricted.

How to Install Full-Spread Sheet Vinyl

Cut the sheet vinyl using the techniques described on page 178 (steps 1 to 5), then lay the sheet vinyl into position, sliding the edges under door casings.

Pull back half of the flooring, then apply a layer of flooring adhesive over the underlayment or old flooring using a ¼" V-notched trowel. Lay the flooring back onto the adhesive.

Roll the bonded section with a weighted floor roller. The roller creates a stronger bond and eliminates air bubbles. Fold over the unbonded section of flooring, apply adhesive, then replace and roll the flooring. Wipe up any adhesive that oozes up around the edges of the vinyl using a damp rag.

Measure and cut metal threshold bars to fit across doorways. Position each bar over the edge of the vinyl flooring and nail it in place.

Vinyl Cove Molding

Vinyl cove molding is popular in basements and other damp locations because it is moisture resistant. The plastic appearance and limited color selection make it less desirable from a design standpoint. Moldings are sold in strips and in rolls and are installed using trowel-on adhesive or adhesive caulk (inset).

To install, apply adhesive to the back side of the vinyl cove molding, not to the installation wall. If you bought your molding in a roll, roll the material out flat and let it rest for at least an hour or two before installing it. After you have applied the molding to the wall, roll the entire molding surface with a J-roller.

Cutting Vinyl Cove Molding

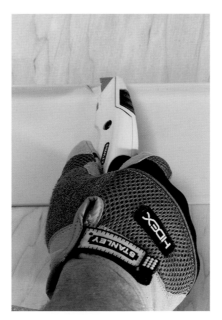

Use a backer board when cutting cove molding. Cut the molding where necessary to fit using a straightedge and sharp utility knife or flooring knife to create a butt joint.

At inside corners, lightly score the back of the molding from top to bottom at the joint of the corner. Notch the base of the molding at the bottom of the score, and press the molding firmly into the corner.

At outside corners, warm the molding with a hair dryer or paint stripping gun, and then fold it so that the back side is exposed, and shave a thin layer off the inside surface. Be careful not to cut all the way through the molding.

Carpet

Carpet remains one of the most popular and versatile of all floor coverings. Almost every home has wall-to-wall carpet in at least a few rooms. It's available in a nearly endless variety of colors, styles, and patterns. It can also be custom-made to express a more personal design. Most carpet is nylon-based, although acrylic and polyester are also popular. Wool carpeting is more formal and more expensive, but also quite popular.

Part of carpet's appeal is its soft texture. Carpet is pleasant to walk on, especially with bare feet, since it's soft and warm underfoot, and is comfortable for children to play on. Because carpet has a pad underneath that acts as a cushion, carpet can also help reduce "floor fatigue."

Carpet also absorbs more noise than other floors, thereby reducing sound between rooms. It also serves as a natural insulator and decreases heat loss through the floor. Wall-to-wall carpet can increase the R-value, or insulation level, of a room.

Carpet offers several universal design advantages. With its non-skid surface, carpet helps reduce falls, which is important for people with limited mobility. Unlike some hard floors, carpet produces no glare, which helps people with vision limitations.

Buying Carpet ▸

When choosing carpet, consider both color and pattern. Lighter shades and colors show dirt and stains more readily, but provide an open, spacious feel. Darker colors and multi-colored patterns don't show as much dirt or wear, but they can also make a room appear smaller.

The materials used in a carpet and its construction can affect the carpet's durability. In high traffic areas, such as hallways and entryways, a top-quality fiber will last longer. Carpet construction, the way in which fibers are attached to the backing, impacts resistance to wear and appearance.

Available widths of certain carpets may affect your buying decision; a roll that's wide enough to cover an entire room eliminates the need for seaming. When seaming is unavoidable, calculate the total square footage to be covered, then add 20 percent to cover trimming and seaming.

The type of carpet you choose will dictate the type of pad you should select. Check carpet sample labels for the manufacturer's recommendations. Since carpet and padding work in tandem to create a floor covering system, install the best pad you can afford that works with your carpet. In addition to making your carpet feel more plush underfoot, the pad makes your floor quieter and warmer. A high-quality pad also helps reduce carpet wear.

Labels on the back of samples usually tell you the carpet's fiber composition, the available widths (usually 12 or 15 feet), what anti-stain treatments and other finishes were applied, and details of the product warranty.

For sheer warmth and comfort underfoot, wall-to-wall carpeting can't be beat. It is a popular flooring choice in basements with concrete floors, but before installing it make sure that you do not have any unresolved moisture or mold problems.

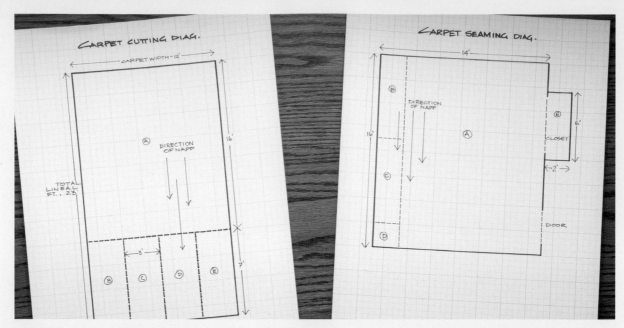

Sketch a scale drawing of the factory carpet roll and another drawing of the room to be carpeted. Use the drawings to plan the cuts and determine how the carpet pieces will be arranged. In most large rooms, the installation will include one large piece of carpet the same width as the factory roll and several smaller pieces that are permanently seamed to the larger piece. When sketching the layout, remember that carpet pieces must be oversized to allow for precise seaming and trimming. Your finished drawings will tell you the length of carpet you need to buy.

Nap slanting away from eye

Nap slanting toward eye

Keep pile direction consistent. Carpet pile is usually slanted, which affects how the carpet looks from different angles as light reflects off the surface. Place seamed pieces so the pile faces the same direction.

Maintain patterns when seaming patterned carpet. Because of this necessity, there's always more waste when installing patterned carpet. For a pattern that repeats itself every 18", for example, each piece must be oversized 18" to ensure the pattern is aligned. Pattern repeat measurements are noted on carpet samples.

At seams, add an extra 3" to each piece when estimating the amount of carpet you'll need. This extra material helps when cutting straight edges for seaming.

At each wall, add 6" for each edge that's along the wall. This surplus will be trimmed away when the carpet is cut to the exact size of the room.

Closet floors are usually covered with a separate piece of carpet that's seamed to the carpet in the main room area.

For stairs, add together the rise and run of each step to estimate the carpet needed for the stairway. Measure the width of the stairway to determine how many strips you can cut from the factory roll. For a 3 ft.-wide stairway, for example, you can cut three strips from a 12 ft.-wide roll, allowing for waste. Rather than seaming carpet strips together end to end, plan the installation so the ends of the strips fall in the stair crotches (see page 207). When possible, try to carpet stairs with a single carpet strip.

Carpet Installation Tools & Materials

Installing carpet requires the use of specialty tools, most notably the knee kicker and power stretcher. These tools are available at most rental centers and carpet stores.

Other than the carpet itself, the pad is the most important material in carpet installation. In addition to making your carpet feel more comfortable, it helps with sound insulation as well. The pad also helps keep warm air from escaping through your floor, thereby keeping the carpet warmer. By cushioning the carpet fibers, the pad reduces wear and extends the life of your carpet. Be sure to use a quality pad.

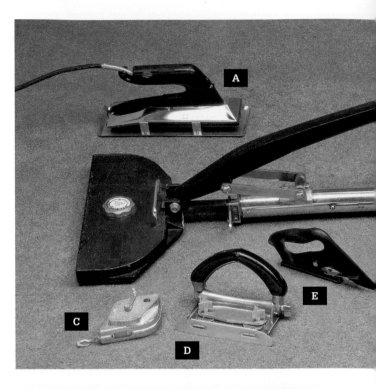

Carpeting tools include: seam iron (A), power stretcher and extensions (B), chalk line (C), edge trimmer (D), row-running knife (E), utility knife (F), stair tool (G), hammer (H), knee kicker (I), aviation snips (J), scissors (K), and stapler (L).

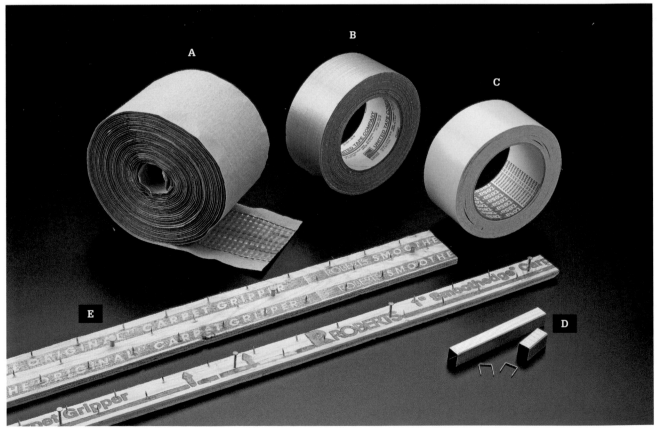

Carpeting materials include hot-glue seam tape (A), used to join carpet pieces together; duct tape (B), for seaming carpet pads; double-sided tape (C), used to secure carpet pads to concrete; staples (D), used to fasten padding to underlayment; and tackless strips (E), for securing the edges of stretched carpet.

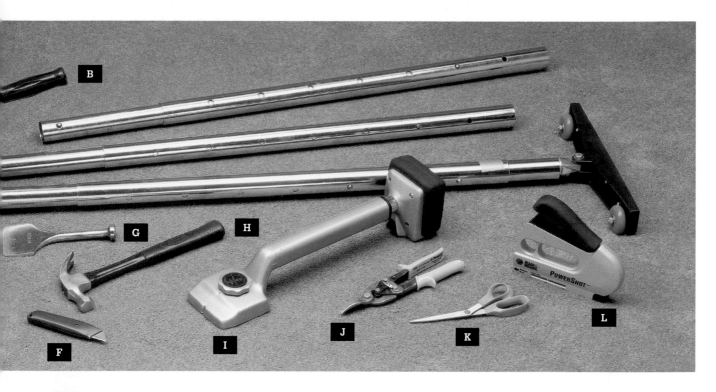

Carpet padding comes in several varieties, including bonded urethane foam (A), cellular sponge rubber (B), grafted prime foam (C), and prime urethane (D). Bonded urethane padding is suitable for low-traffic areas, while prime urethane and grafted prime foam are better for high-traffic areas. In general, cut pile, cut-and-loop, and high-level loop carpets perform best with prime or bonded urethane or rubber pads that are less than 7/16" thick. For Berbers or other stiff-backed carpets, use 3/8"-thick bonded urethane foam or cellular sponge rubber. Foam padding is graded by density: the denser the foam, the better the pad. Rubber padding is graded by weight: the heavier, the better.

Using Carpet Tools

The knee kicker and power stretcher are the two most important tools for installing carpet. They are used to stretch a carpet smooth and taut before securing it to tackless strips installed around the perimeter of a room.

The power stretcher is the more efficient of the two tools and should be used to stretch and secure as much of the carpet as possible. The knee kicker is used to secure carpet in tight areas where the power stretcher can't reach, such as closets.

A logical stretching sequence is essential to good carpet installation. Begin by attaching the carpet at a doorway or corner, then use the power stretcher and knee kicker to stretch the carpet away from the attached areas and toward the opposite walls.

Understanding how to use specialized tools, such as the knee kicker, is essential to a successful installation.

How to Use a Knee Kicker

A knee kicker has teeth that grab the carpet foundation for stretching. Adjust the depth of the teeth by turning the knob on the knee kicker head. The teeth should be set deep enough to grab the carpet foundation without penetrating to the padding.

Place the kicker head a few inches away from the wall to avoid dislodging the tackless strips, then strike the kicker cushion firmly with your knee, stretching the carpet taut. Tack the carpet to the pins on the tackless strips to hold it in place.

How to Use a Power Stretcher

Align the pieces of the power stretcher along the floor with the tail positioned at a point where the carpet is already secured and the head positioned just short of the opposite wall. Fit the ends of the sections together.

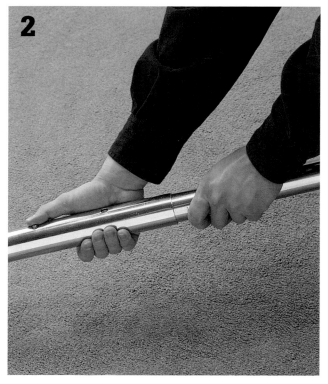

Telescope one or more of the extension poles until the tail rests against the starting wall or block and the head is about 5" from the opposite wall.

Adjust the teeth on the head so they grip the carpet foundation (see step 1, opposite page). Depress the lever on the head to stretch the carpet. The stretcher head should move the carpet about 2".

Installing Carpet Transitions

Doorways, entryways, and other transition areas require special treatment when installing carpet. Transition materials and techniques vary, depending on the level and type of the adjoining flooring.

For a transition to a floor that's the same height or lower than the bottom of the carpet, attach a metal carpet bar to the floor and secure the carpet inside the bar. This transition is often used where carpet meets a vinyl or tile floor. Carpet bars are sold in standard door-width lengths and in longer strips.

For a transition to a floor that's higher than the carpet bottom, use tackless strips, as if the adjoining floor surface was a wall. This transition is common where carpet meets a hardwood floor.

For a transition to another carpet of the same height, join the two carpet sections together with hot-glue seam tape.

For a transition in a doorway between carpets of different heights or textures, install tackless strips and a hardwood threshold (below). Thresholds are available predrilled and ready to install with screws.

Metal carpet bar

Tackless strip tuck-under

Hot-glue seam tape

Hardwood threshold

How to Make Transitions with Metal Carpet Bars

Measure and cut a carpet bar to fit the threshold using a hacksaw. Nail the carpet bar in place. In doorways, the upturned metal flange should lie directly under the center of the door when it's closed.

Roll out, cut, and seam the carpet. Fold the carpet back in the transition area, then mark it for trimming. The edge of the carpet should fall ⅛ to ¼" short of the corner of the carpet bar so it can be stretched into the bar.

Use a knee kicker to stretch the carpet snugly into the corner of the carpet bar. Press the carpet down onto the pins with a stair tool. Bend the carpet bar flange down over the carpet by striking it with a hammer and a block of wood.

How to Make Transitions with Tackless Strips

Install a tackless strip, leaving a gap equal to ⅔ the thickness of the carpet for trimming. Roll out, cut, and seam the carpet. Mark the edge of the carpet between the tackless strip and the adjoining floor surface about ⅛" past the point where it meets the adjacent floor.

Use a straightedge and utility knife to trim the excess carpet. Stretch the carpet toward the strip with a knee kicker, then press it onto the pins of the tackless strip.

Tuck the edge of the carpet into the gap between the tackless strip and the existing floor using a stair tool.

How to Install Tackless Strips

Starting in a corner, nail tackless strips to the floor, keeping a gap between the strips and the walls that's about ⅔ the thickness of the carpet. Use plywood spacers to maintain the gap. Angled pins on the strip should point toward the wall.

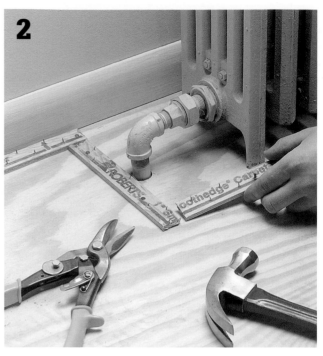

Use aviation snips to cut tackless strips to fit around radiators, door moldings, and other obstacles.

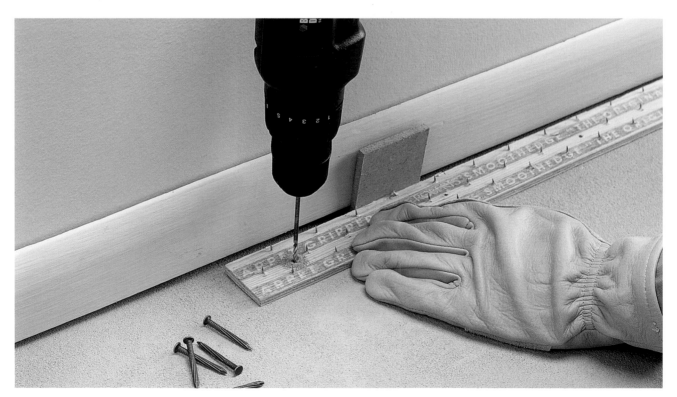

Variation: On concrete, use wider tackless strips. Using a masonry bit, drill pilot holes through the strips and into the floor. Then fasten the strips with 1½" fluted masonry nails.

How to Install Carpet Padding

Roll out enough padding to cover the entire floor. Make sure the seams between the padding are tight. If one face of the padding has a slicker surface, keep the slick surface face up, making it easier to slide the carpet over the pad during installation.

Use a utility knife to cut away excess padding along the edges. The padding should touch, but not overlap, the tackless strips.

Tape the seams together with duct tape, then staple the padding to the floor every 12".

Variation: To fasten padding to a concrete floor, apply double-sided tape next to the tackless strips, along the seams, and in an "X" pattern across the floor.

How to Cut & Seam Carpet

1

Position the carpet roll against one wall, with its loose end extending up the wall about 6", then roll out the carpet until it reaches the opposite wall.

2

At the opposite wall, mark the back of the carpet at each edge about 6" beyond the point where the carpet touches the wall. Pull the carpet back away from the wall so the marks are visible.

Variation: When cutting loop-pile carpet, avoid severing the loops by cutting it from the top side using a row-running knife. Fold the carpet back along the cut line to part the pile (left) and make a crease along the part line. Lay the carpet flat and cut along the part in the pile (right). Cut slowly to ensure a smooth, straight cut.

3

Snap a chalk line across the back of the carpet between the marks. Place a scrap piece of plywood under the cutting area to protect the carpet and padding from the knife blade. Cut along the line using a straightedge and utility knife.

4

Next to walls, straddle the edge of the carpet and nudge it with your foot until it extends up the wall by about 6" and is parallel to the wall.

5

At the corners, relieve buckling by slitting the carpet with a utility knife, allowing the carpet to lie somewhat flat. Make sure that corner cuts do not cut into usable carpet.

6

Using your seaming plan as a guide, measure and cut fill-in pieces of carpet to complete the installation. Be sure to include a 6" surplus at each wall and a 3" surplus on each edge that will be seamed to another piece of carpet. Set the cut pieces in place, making sure the pile faces in the same direction on all pieces.

(continued)

7

Roll back the large piece of carpet on the side to be seamed, then use a chalk line to snap a straight seam edge about 2" from the factory edge. Keep the ends of the line about 18" from the sides of the carpet where the overlap onto the walls causes the carpet to buckle.

8

Using a straightedge and utility knife, carefully cut the carpet along the chalk line. To extend the cutting lines to the edges of the carpet, pull the corners back at an angle so they lie flat, then cut the line with the straightedge and utility knife. Place scrap wood under the cutting area to protect the carpet while cutting.

9

On smaller carpet pieces, cut straight seam edges where the small pieces will be joined to one another. Don't cut the edges that will be seamed to the large carpet piece until after the small pieces are joined together.

Option: Apply a continuous bead of seam glue along the cut edges of the backing at seams to ensure that the carpet will not fray.

Plug in the seam iron and set it aside to heat up, then measure and cut hot-glue seam tape for all seams. Begin by joining the small fill-in pieces to form one large piece. Center the tape under the seam with the adhesive side facing up.

Set the iron under the carpet at one end of the tape until the adhesive liquifies, usually about 30 seconds. Working in 12" sections, slowly move the iron along the tape, letting the carpet fall onto the hot adhesive behind it. Set weights at the end of the seam to hold the pieces in place.

(continued)

Press the edges of the carpet together into the melted adhesive behind the iron. Separate the pile with your fingers to make sure no fibers are stuck in the glue and the seam is tight, then place a weighted board over the seam to keep it flat while the glue sets.

Variation: To close any gaps in loop-pile carpet seams, use a knee kicker to gently push the seam edges together while the adhesive is still hot.

Continue seaming the fill-in pieces together. When the tape's adhesive has cooled, turn the seamed piece over and cut a fresh seam edge as done in steps 7 and 8. Reheat and remove about 1½" of tape from the end of each seam to keep it from overlapping the tape on the large piece.

14

Use hot-glue seam tape to join the seamed pieces to the large piece of carpet, repeating steps 10 through 12.

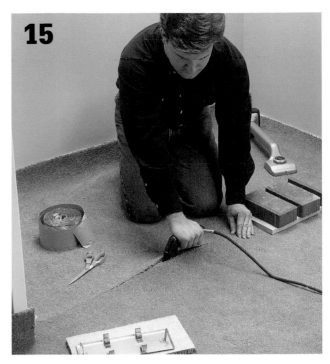

15

If you're laying carpet in a closet, cut a fill-in piece and join it to the main carpet with hot-glue seam tape.

16

At radiators, pipes, and other obstructions, cut slits in the carpet with a utility knife. Cut long slits from the edge of the carpet to the obstruction, then cut short cross-slits where the carpet will fit around the obstruction.

Partition Walls ▸

To fit carpet around partition walls where the edges of the wall or door jamb meet the floor, make diagonal cuts from the edge of the carpet at the center of the wall to the points where the edges of the wall meet the floor.

How to Stretch & Secure Carpet

Before stretching the seamed carpet, read through this entire section and create a stretching sequence similar to the one shown here. Start by fastening the carpet at a doorway threshold using carpet transitions (see pages 192 to 193).

If the doorway is close to a corner, use the knee kicker to secure the carpet to the tackless strips between the door and the corner. Also secure a few feet of carpet along the adjacent wall, working toward the corner.

Use a power stretcher to stretch the carpet toward the wall opposite the door. Brace the tail with a length of 2 × 4 placed across the doorway. Leaving the tail in place and moving only the stretcher head, continue stretching and securing the carpet along the wall, working toward the nearest corner in 12 to 24" increments.

As you stretch the carpet, secure it onto the tackless strips with a stair tool and hammer.

With the power stretcher still extended from the doorway to the opposite side of the room, knee-kick the carpet onto the tackless strips along the closest wall, starting near the corner closest to the stretcher tail. Disengage and move the stretcher only if it's in the way.

Reposition the stretcher so its tail is against the center of the wall you just secured. Stretch and secure the carpet along the opposite wall, working from the center toward a corner. If there's a closet in an adjacent wall, work toward that wall, not the closet.

(continued)

7

Use the knee kicker to stretch and secure the carpet inside the closet (if necessary). Stretch and fasten the carpet against the back wall first, then do the side walls. After the carpet in the closet is stretched and secured, use the knee kicker to secure the carpet along the walls next to the closet. Disengage the power stretcher only if it's in the way.

8

Return the head of the power stretcher to the center of the wall. Finish securing carpet along this wall, working toward the other corner of the room.

9

Reposition the stretcher to secure the carpet along the last wall of the room, working from the center toward the corners. The tail block should be braced against the opposite wall.

10

Use a carpet edge trimmer to trim surplus carpet away from the walls. At corners, use a utility knife to finish the cuts.

Making Cutouts ▶

Locate any floor vents under the stretched carpet, then use a utility knife to cut away the carpet, starting at the center. It's important that this be done only after the stretching is complete.

11

Tuck the trimmed edges of the carpet neatly into the gaps between the tackless strips and the walls using a stair tool and hammer.

How to Install Carpet on Stairs

Measure the stairway. Measure the width and add together the vertical rise and horizontal run of the steps to determine how much carpet you'll need. Use a straightedge and utility knife to carefully cut the carpet to the correct dimensions.

Fasten tackless strips to the risers and the treads. On the risers, place the strips about 1" above the treads. On the treads, place the strips about ¾" from the risers. Make sure the pins point toward the crotch of the step. On the bottom riser, leave a gap equal to ⅔ the carpet thickness.

For each step, cut a piece of carpet padding the width of the step and long enough to cover the tread and a few inches of the riser below it. Staple the padding in place.

Position the carpet on the stairs with the pile direction pointing down. Secure the bottom edge using a stair tool to tuck the end of the carpet between the tackless strip and the floor.

Use a knee kicker and stair tool to stretch the carpet onto the tackless strip on the first tread. Start in the center of the step, then alternate kicks on either side until the carpet is completely secured on the step.

Use a hammer and stair tool to wedge the carpet firmly into the back corner of the step. Repeat this process for each step.

Where two carpet pieces meet, secure the edge of the upper piece first, then stretch and secure the lower piece.

Carpet Squares

Most carpeting has a single design and is stretched from wall to wall. It covers more square feet of American homes than any other material. You can install it yourself, following the instructions on pages 184 to 207. But if you want a soft floor covering that gives you more options, carpet squares are an excellent choice.

Manufacturers have found ways to create attractive new carpet using recycled fibers. This not only reuses material that would otherwise become landfill, it reduces waste in manufacturing as well. So, instead of adding to problems of resource consumption and pollution, carpet squares made from recycled materials help reduce them.

The squares are attached to each other and to the floor with adhesive dots. They can be installed on most clean, level, dry underlayment or onto an existing floor. If the surface underneath is waxed or varnished, check with the manufacturer before you use any adhesives on it.

Tools & Materials ▸

Adhesive	Marking pen or pencil
Carpenter's square	Measuring tape
Chalk line	Straightedge
Cleaning supplies	Carpet squares
Craft/utility knife	Scrap plywood

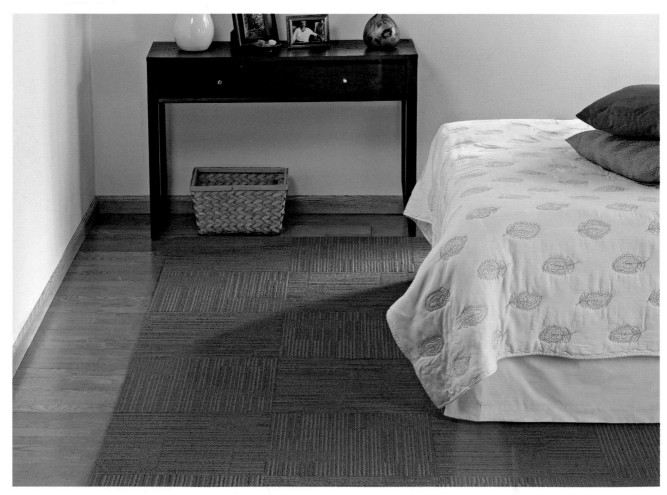

Carpet tiles combine the warmth and comfort of carpet with do-it-yourself installation, custom designs, and easy replacement. They can be laid wall-to-wall or in an area rug style, as shown above.

How to Install Carpet Squares

1

Take the squares out of the package. Usually, you want to keep new flooring out of the way until you're ready to install it. But some materials, such as carpet or sheet vinyl, should be at room temperature for at least 12 hours before you lay them down.

2

Check the requirements for the recommended adhesive. You can install carpet squares over many other flooring materials, including hardwood, laminates, and resilient sheets or tiles. The carpet squares shown here are fastened with adhesive dots, so almost any existing floor will provide a usable surface.

3

Make sure the existing floor is clean, smooth, stable, and dry. Use floor leveler if necessary to eliminate any hills or valleys. If any part of the floor is loose, secure it to the subfloor or underlayment before you install the carpet squares. Vacuum the surface and wipe it with a damp cloth.

4

Snap chalk lines between diagonally opposite corners to find the center point for the room. In rooms with unusual shapes, determine the visual center and mark it. Next, snap chalk lines across the center and perpendicular to the walls. This set of guidelines will show you where to start.

(continued)

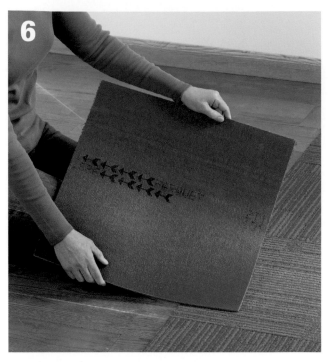

Lay a base row of carpet squares on each side of the two guidelines. When you reach the walls, make note of how much you will need to cut. You should have the same amount to cut on each side. If not, adjust the center point and realign the squares.

Check the backs of the squares before you apply any adhesive. They should indicate a direction, using arrows or other marks, so that the finished pile has a consistent appearance. If you plan to mix colors, this is the time to establish your pattern.

Fasten the base rows in place using the manufacturer's recommended adhesive. This installation calls for two adhesive dots per square. As you place each square, make sure it is aligned with the guidelines and fits tightly against the next square.

When you reach a wall, flip the last square over. Push it against the wall until it is snug. If you are planning a continuous pattern, align the arrows with the existing squares. If you are creating a parquet pattern, turn the new square 90 degrees before marking it.

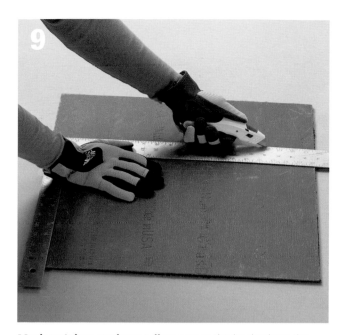

Mark notches or draw a line across the back where the new square overlaps the next-to-last one. Using a sharp utility knife, a carpenter's square, and a tough work surface, cut along this line. The cut square should fit neatly in the remaining space.

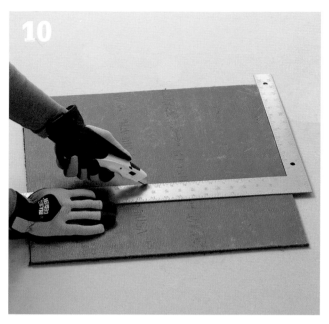

At a door jamb, place a square face up where it will go. Lean the square against the jamb and mark the point where they meet. Move the square to find the other cutline, and mark that as well. Flip the square over, mark the two lines using a carpenter's square, and cut out the corner.

Finish all four base rows before you fill in the rest of the room. As you work, check the alignment of each row. If you notice a row going out of line, find the point where the direction changed, then remove squares back to that point and start again.

Work outward from the center so that you have a known reference for keeping rows straight. Save the cut pieces from the ends. They may be useful for patching odd spaces around doorways, heat registers, radiator pipes, and when you reach the corners.

Finishes & Surface Treatments

One of the most desirable features of hardwood flooring is that it's a natural product, with grain patterns that are interesting to the eye and a combination of colors that gives any room a soft, inviting glow. The resilience of wood fibers makes a hardwood floor extremely durable, but they are susceptible to changes caused by moisture and aging.

Typically, the first thing to wear out on a hardwood floor is the finish. Refinishing the floor by sanding it with a rented drum sander and applying a topcoat, such as polyurethane, will make your old floor look new. If you want to retain the floor's aged glow without sanding, or if the boards have been sanded before and are less than ⅜ inches thick, consider stripping the floor.

Once your floor is finished, you may want to dress it up with a favorite design, border, or pattern. If the wood will not look good refinished, consider painting it. Pages 214 to 217 offer exciting ways to customize your wood floor.

In this chapter:

- Floor Stains & Finishes
- Painting Wood Floors
- Finishing Concrete Floors
- Refinishing Hardwood Floors

Floor Stains & Finishes

A stain is applied to the surface of an unfinished wood floor to change the color to a variety of natural wood tones. Colored stains can also be applied to previously stained and finished floors for a colorwashed effect. Consider a colored stain to complement your décor; green blends well with a rustic decorating scheme and white adds to a contemporary look.

Look for a water-based stain that's formulated for easy application without lap marks or streaking. Conditioners can help prevent streaking and control grain raise when you're using water-based wood stains. Use a wood conditioner on the wood prior to staining, if recommended by the manufacturer.

You can also stain wood by colorwashing it with diluted latex paint. The colorwash solution will be considerably lighter in color than the original paint color. Use one part latex paint and four parts water to make a colorwash solution, and experiment with small amounts of paint until you achieve the desired color. Apply the stain or colorwash solution in an inconspicuous area, such as a closet, to test the application method and color before staining the entire floor surface.

Aged finishes (see page 217) give floors timeworn character which is especially suitable for a rustic or transitional decorating style. Although they appear distressed and fragile, these finishes are actually very durable. Aged finishes are especially suitable on previously painted or stained floors, but they may also be applied to new or resurfaced wood flooring. Up to three coats of paint in different colors may be used.

Tools & Materials ▸

Synthetic brush
Sponge applicators
Rubber gloves
Paint pad and
   pole extension
Power sander
Fine- and medium-
   grit sandpaper
Vacuum
Tack cloth

Water-based stain
   or latex paint
High-gloss and satin
   clear finishes
Latex enamel paints
Paint roller
Hammer
Chisel
Awl

Applying wood stain is a great way to draw attention to the material's naturally beautiful texture and coloring.

Wood Stain Variations

Dark wood tones work well for traditional rooms. White colorwashing over a previously dark-stained floor mellows the formal appearance.

Medium, warm wood tones have a casual appearance. White colorwashing over a medium wood tone results in an antiqued look.

Pale neutral stains are often used for contemporary rooms. A blue colorwash can give a pale floor bold new character.

How to Apply a Stained Finish to a Bare Wood Floor

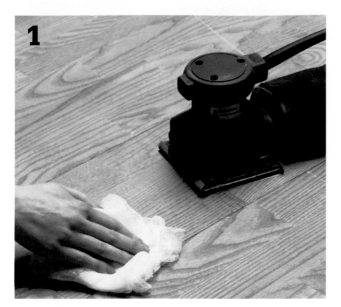

Sand the floor surface with fine-grit sandpaper in the direction of the wood grain. Remove the sanding dust with a vacuum, then wipe the floor with a tack cloth.

Prepare and apply stain. Wear rubber gloves when working with any stain product. Stir the stain or colorwash solution thoroughly. Apply the stain or solution to the floor using a synthetic brush or sponge applicator. Work on one small section at a time. Keep a wet edge and avoid overlapping the brush strokes.

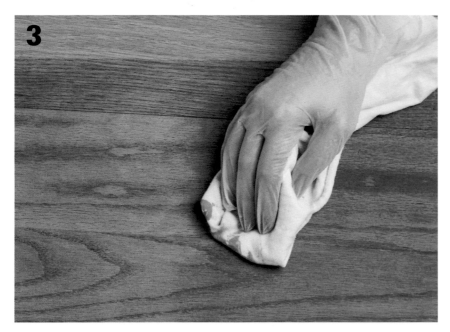

Wipe away excess stain after the waiting time recommended by the manufacturer using a dry, lint-free rag. Wipe across the grain of the wood first, then wipe with the grain. Continue applying and wiping stain until the entire floor is finished. Allow the stain to dry. Sand the floor lightly, using fine-grit sandpaper, then remove any sanding dust with a tack cloth. For a deeper color, apply a second coat of stain and allow it to dry thoroughly.

Apply a coat of high-gloss clear finish to the stained floor using a sponge applicator or a paint pad with pole extension. Allow the finish to dry. Sand the floor lightly, using fine-grit sandpaper, then wipe with a tack cloth. Apply two coats of satin clear finish following manufacturer's directions.

How to Apply an Aged & Distressed Finish

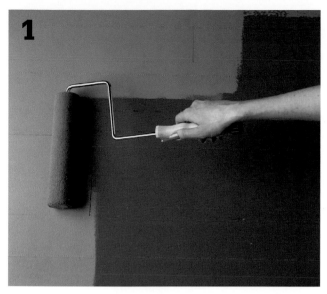

1

Finish the floor with a painted or stained base coat. Sand the floor lightly, using fine-grit sandpaper. Vacuum the floor and wipe away dust with a tack cloth. Apply two or three coats of enamel using a different color of paint for each coat. Allow the floor to dry between coats. Sand the floor lightly between coats, using fine-grit sandpaper, and wipe away dust with a tack cloth.

2

Use a power sander to sand the floor surface with medium-grit sandpaper, sanding harder in some areas to remove the top and middle coats of paint. Avoid sanding beyond the base coat of paint or stain.

3

To distress the floor further, hit the wood with the head of a hammer or a chain. Gouge the boards with a chisel, or pound holes randomly using an awl. Create as many imperfections as desired, then sand the floor lightly with fine-grit sandpaper. Apply two coats of satin clear finish, allowing the floor to dry completely between coats.

Creative Color Options ▸

Two coats of dark green paint were applied over a previously stained floor. Sanding revealed the stain in some areas. The floor was further distressed using a hammer, chisel, and awl.

Maroon base coat and light rose top coat were painted over a previously stained floor. Sanding created an aged look suitable for a cottage bedroom.

Painting Wood Floors

Paint is a quick, cost-effective way to cover up wood floors that no longer look their best, but a floor doesn't have to be distressed or damaged to benefit from paint. Floors in perfect condition in both formal and informal spaces can be decorated with paint to add color and personality. For example, one could unify a space by extending a painted floor through a hallway to a staircase. Stencil designs or faux finishes can make an oversized room feel cozy and inviting. There are even techniques for disguising worn spots. In addition, paint is a relatively inexpensive flooring finish if your budget is tight.

Tools & Materials ▸

Lacquer thinner	Nail set
Primer	Dust mask
Latex paint specifically for floors	Fine- and medium-grit sandpaper
Wide painter's tape	Broom
Paint roller and tray	Vacuum
4"-wide paintbrush	Tack cloth
Extension pole	Stir sticks
Paint scraper	Paint can opener
Hammer	Polyurethane sealer
Pole sander	Paint pad
Putty knife	Straightedge

Rev up a worn-out floor with a bright paint color. Paint can not only disguise flaws, but it can also add warmth and character to a room.

How to Paint Wood Floors

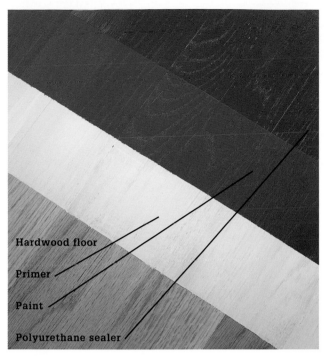

Hardwood floor
Primer
Paint
Polyurethane sealer

To paint a wood floor you must apply primer first, then apply the paint, and follow that with a polyurethane sealer. Make sure the products you choose are made specifically for floors.

1

Use a paint scraper to smooth rough spots. Use a pole sander to sand with the grain of the wood. For coarse wood, use medium-grit sandpaper. Scuff glossy hardwoods with fine sandpaper (120-grit) for good adhesion.

2

Clean up dust with a broom or vacuum. Use a damp cloth to remove fine dust. Use a cloth dampened with lacquer thinner for a final cleaning. If you see any nails sticking up, tap them down with a hammer and nail set.

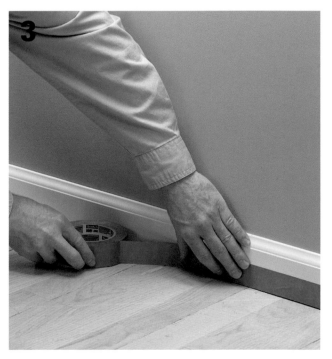

3

Protect the baseboards with wide painter's tape. Press the tape edges down so paint doesn't seep underneath.

(continued)

Mix primer well (see step 5 for mixing technique). Use a 4"-wide brush to apply the primer around the perimeter of the room. Then paint the remaining floor with a roller on an extension pole. Allow the primer to dry.

To mix paint, pour half of the paint into another can, stirring the paint in both containers with a wooden stir stick before recombining them. As you stir, you want a smooth consistency.

Paint. Use a 4" brush to apply a paint around the border. To paint the rest of the floor, use a roller on an extension pole. Always roll from a dry area to a wet area to minimize lap lines. Allow paint to dry. Apply second coat of paint. Allow to dry.

Apply 2 or 3 coats of a matte-finish, waterbased polyurethane sealer using a painting pad on a pole. Allow the paint to dry. Sand with a pole sander using fine sandpaper. Clean up dust with a tack cloth.

How to Paint a Checkerboard Floor

If your wood floor is in poor condition, it can be camouflaged with a design, such as a classic checkerboard pattern. Proper preparation is essential for lasting results. If you've already painted the floor based on the instructions from the first half of this project, you are well on your way and you have the base color already painted. You just have to paint in the darker colored squares.

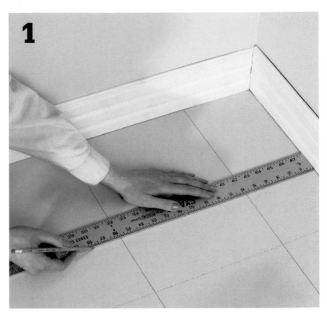

Measure the entire floor. Now, determine the size of squares you'll use. Plan the design so the areas of the floor with the highest visibility, such as the main entrance, have full squares. Place partial squares along the walls in less conspicuous areas. Mark the design lines on the floor using a straightedge and pencil.

Using painter's tape, outline the squares that are to remain light in color. Press firmly along all edges of the tape using a putty knife to create a tight seal.

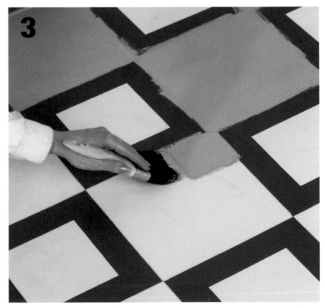

Paint the remaining squares with the darker paint color. Paint small areas at a time. Once you have painted the entire box and a few surrounding boxes, remove the masking tape from the painted squares. Be sure to remove the tape before the paint completely dries. After all of the paint has completely dried, apply a coat of high-gloss clear finish using a paint roller or paint pad with a pole extension. Allow the finish to dry.

Finishing Concrete Floors

If your concrete floor is not perfectly dry, smooth, and in good repair, you have several options for improving it. A simple cleaning is the easiest and most obvious solution. For concrete floors, a process called etching can be done in conjunction with basic cleaning. Etching uses mild acid to remove oil, grime, and other stains detergent won't take care of. Etching is recommended as a preparatory treatment for applying paint or acid-based stain. Prior to etching, any pre-existing paint must be completely removed and any minor cracks or imperfections should be repaired.

Once the concrete floor is repaired, cleaned, and etched, you may choose simply to seal it. There is some debate about the advisability of sealing concrete—sealing products remove the concrete's natural ability to breathe, which can lead to problems related to moisture entrapment. But because concrete floors receive so much traffic and filth, it is generally agreed that a seal coat is a definite aid in ongoing maintenance.

After etching, but before sealing, is the time to paint (or you can use an acid-based stain if you wish). To paint an etched concrete floor, use a two-part, epoxy-based product that you mix together before application. The paint can be applied with ordinary brushes and rollers. Each gallon will cover approximately 250 square feet and dries in about 48 hours. When fully cured, the paint will resist oil, brake fluids, and other automotive chemicals.

Tools & Materials ▸

Stiff-bristle push broom	Baking soda
Long-handled paint roller or squeegee	Pressure washer
	Shop vacuum
Protective glasses	Power buffer
Plastic sheeting and tape	Garden hose
Cleaning and finishing products	Painter's tape
	Paintbrush
Pump sprayer or plastic watering can	Boots
	Respirator
Large plastic bucket	Detergent
Stiff-bristle brush	Muriatic acid
Antiskid additive	Rubber gloves
Two-part epoxy floor paint	Clear sealer
Drill with mixing paddle attachment	Stir sticks

Specially formulated epoxy-based paint will give your concrete floor a low-cost facelift and comes in a variety of colors from which you can choose.

Tools & Materials for Painting Concrete Floors

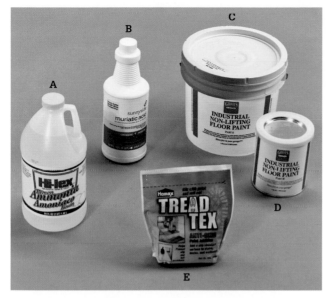

Preparation and finishing materials include: ammonia-based detergent for general cleaning of concrete surface (A); muriatic acid for final cleaning immediately before paint application (B); two-part epoxy floor paint Part A (C); two-part epoxy floor paint Part B (D); antiskid granular additive (optional) (E).

A power washer does a fast and thorough job of cleaning dirty concrete floors prior to painting. Use tools like this with caution. If handled carelessly, they are powerful enough to create more mess than they remove.

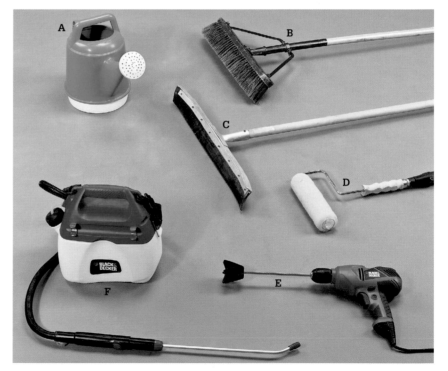

A power scrubber/buffer can be rented to clean dirty, oily floors and to help work floor treatment products into the concrete surface. These can be tricky to handle at first, so it's a good idea to practice with plain water before you use the scrubber with chemicals.

General purpose tools that are useful in a floor maintenance and painting project include: a plastic watering can for broadcasting cleaning and finishing chemicals (A); a push broom (B); a long-handled squeegee (C); a long-handled paint roller (D); a drill outfitted with a paddle-type mixing attachment (E); a plastic-body garden sprayer for applying chemical treatments (F).

How to Clean & Etch a Concrete Floor

Testing Tip ▸

Test the floor to make sure moisture is not migrating up from below. Tape a large piece of plastic to the floor and let it rest overnight. If condensation forms on the underside of the plastic it means that transpiration is occurring and the paint will likely fail. Test the floor more than once and in multiple spots to be sure of its suitability for paint.

Rinse the floor thoroughly after sweeping or vacuuming. A simple garden hose can be used for this process, or you can employ a pressure washer for deep cleaning. Use grease-cutting detergent and also scrub with a stiff-bristle brush as necessary to remove oily stains.

Prepare the acid-based etching solution by pouring one cup of muriatic acid into a pump sprayer or a plastic watering can containing clean water for the recommended dilution ratio (see acid container label). Always add acid to water: never add water to acid. *Caution: Follow the safety precautions on the acid product container at all times.*

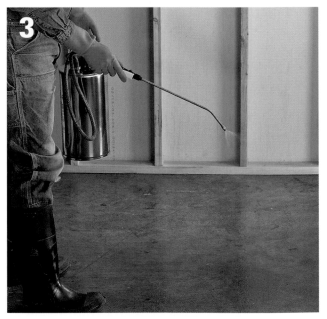

Broadcast the etching solution with a sprayer or a watering can. Apply it evenly in areas small enough that they will not dry before you can work the acid into the concrete surface (100 sq. ft. at a time is a good guideline).

Work the acid solution into the floor surface with a stiff-bristle push broom or a power buffer. Let the acid solution rest for 5 to 10 minutes. A mild foaming action indicates that the product is working.

Neutralize the acid by brushing the floor with a solution of baking soda dissolved in water (1 cup per gallon of water)only after all of the floor surface has been etched.

Rinse the concrete floor thoroughly with a hose and clean water, or with a pressure washer. Rinse multiple times for best results.

Vacuum the wet floor thoroughly with a wet/dry shop vacuum after you have finished rinsing it. Vacuuming will help prevent any residue from forming on the floor when it dries.

How to Seal a Concrete Floor

Once etched, clean, and dry, your concrete is ready for clear sealer or liquid repellent. Mix the sealer in a bucket with a stir stick. Lay painter's tape down for a testing patch. Apply sealer to this area and allow to dry to ensure desired appearance. Concrete sealers tend to make the surface slick when wet. Add an antiskid additive to aid with traction, especially on stairs.

Apply wide painter's tape to protect walls, and then use a good-quality 4"-wide paintbrush to coat the perimeter with sealer.

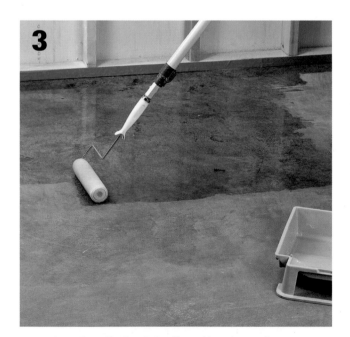

Use a long-handled paint roller with at least ½" nap to apply an even coat to the rest of the surface. Do small sections at a time (about 2 × 3 ft.). Work in one orientation (e.g., north to south). Avoid lap marks by always maintaining a wet edge. Do not work the area once the coating has partially dried; this could cause it to lift from the surface.

Allow the surface to dry according to the manufacturer's instructions, usually 8 to 12 hours minimum. Then apply a second coat in the opposite direction of the first coat. If the first coat was north to south, the second coat should be east to west.

How to Paint a Concrete Floor

1

Mix the first part (Part A) of the two-part epoxy paint. Following the instructions on the can label precisely, add the Part B liquid to the Part A and blend with a mixing paddle attachment mounted in an electric drill. If you plan to add antiskid granules, add them at this point and mix them in well.

2

Paint the perimeter of the room with a large brush, making sure to get paint all the way into the corners and up against the bottom of the walls. Feather the paint out on the room side so you do not leave any ridges that will show.

3

Paint the floor with a long-handled roller extension and a short-nap sleeve. Don't make the coat too thick; a couple of thin coats is much better than one thick one. Once you have completed the first coat, close all doors and do not open them until the paint has dried. Sweep or vacuum the floor after the first coat (the primer coat) dries. Wear clean shoes and try and get up as much debris as you can.

4

Apply the second coat of paint in the same manner as you applied the first. Instructions may vary, but in general it isn't a good idea to apply more than two coats. Reserve any leftover paint for occasional touch-ups in high-wear areas.

Refinishing Hardwood Floors

Making worn and dull hardwood floors look new again dramatically improves the appearance of a home. And the fact that very old hardwood floors can be completely restored to showroom condition is one of their real advantages over other types of flooring. Refinishing floors is time-consuming, messy, and disruptive to your household routine. Depending on the size of the room, be prepared to devote at least a weekend to this project.

If you don't want to complete the entire job yourself, you can still save money by doing some of the prep work yourself. Professionals often add on additional fees for removing and replacing shoe molding (see page 231), nailing or gluing down loose boards (page 239), filling gouges and dents with wood putty (page 239), setting protruding nails, putting up plastic (page 230), cleaning the floor, and even moving furniture.

Note: If your floors are less than ½-inch thick, you should consult a floor contractor to see if the floors can withstand the refinishing process.

Tools & Materials ▸

Paint tray	5" random
Paint brush	orbital sander
Painting pad	Sandpaper in
Pry bar	multiple grades
Wood shims	Broom and/
Painter's tape	or vacuum
Nail set	Tack cloth and
Hammer	clean rags
Rotary buffer	Polyurethane finish
Sanding block	Fine and medium
Paint scraper	abrasive pad
Extension pole	Eye and ear
Power edge sander	protection
Power drum sander	Dust mask
Scrap 2 × 4 lumber	or respirator

Reviving your hardwood floors is definitely worth the hard work. After refinishing a tired-looking floor you will realize why hardwood floors are so durable and long-lasting: they clean up beautifully.

Tools & Materials for Refinishing Hardwood Floors

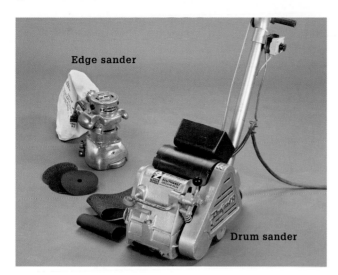

Edge sander

Drum sander

Specialty tools and products are necessary for resurfacing or refinishing wood floors. If several scratches, gouges, and stains have damaged the floor, it may be a good idea to resurface it by sanding using a drum sander for the main floor area and an edger sander for areas next to baseboards. Both tools can be rented from home improvement or rental centers. As a general rule, use the finest-grit sandpaper that's effective for the job. Be sure to get complete operating and safety instructions when renting these tools.

Types of Wood Finishes ▸

Surface finish—A floor finish applied to the wood surface, providing a harder and more durable coating than a sealer with a wax covering. For example, polyurethane (oil- or water-based), varnish, shellac, and lacquer.

Penetrant finish—Penetrant floor finishes seep into the wood pores and become an integral part of the wood (stains or sealers).

Stains—Penetrants that alter the natural color of the wood. They can be used with a surface finish or protected with a sealer and wax.

Sealers—Either clear or tinted penetrants that need to be protected with a wax or surface finish.

Wax—Wood floors not protected with a surface finish need to be covered with a coat of liquid, non-waterbased wax. Wax is not as durable as surface finish; periodically, it must be reapplied. The advantage is that patched areas easily blend in.

Tools & materials include: paint tray (A), polyurethane (B), dust masks (C), tack cloth (D), random orbital sander (E), painter's plastic (F), paint scraper (G), paint pad (H), prybar (I), push broom (J), eye protection (K), zip door (L), sandpaper (M), painter's tape (N), sanding block (O), kneepads (P), stapler (Q), paintbrush (R), broom (S), hammer (T), dustpan (U), nail set (V).

Preparing to Refinish a Hardwood Floor

Staple plastic on all doorways. Place a zip door over the entryway you plan to use for the duration of the project.

Use painter's tape and plastic to cover heating and cooling registers, ceiling fans, and light fixtures.

Safety Tip ▸

Even with proper ventilation, inhaling sawdust is a health risk. We recommend getting a respirator for a project like this. If you don't use one, you must at least wear a dust mask. Eye protection is also a must; and you'll thank yourself for buying a good pair of strong work gloves—they make the sander vibrations a little more bearable.

Important! Always unplug the sander whenever loading or unloading sandpaper.

Place a fan in a nearby window to blow the circulating dust outside.

How to Refinish a Hardwood Floor

Wedge a pry bar between the shoe molding and baseboards. Move along the wall as nails loosen. Once removed, place a scrap 2 × 4 board against the wall and, pry out baseboard at nails (inset). Maintain the gap with wood shims. Number the sections for easy replacement. Place wide masking tape along the baseboards. Drive protruding nails in the floor ⅛" below the surface with a nail set.

Practice with the drum sander turned off. Move forward and backward. Tilt or raise it off the floor a couple of times. A drum sander is heavy, bulky, and awkward. Once it touches the floor, it walks forward; if you stop it, it gouges the floor.

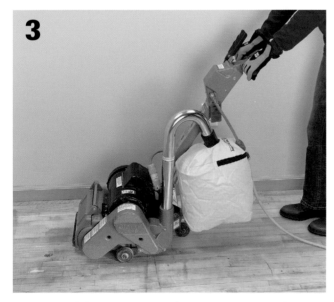

For the initial pass with the drum sander, sand with the grain using 40- or 60-grit paper; if there are large scratches, use 20 or 30. Start two-thirds down the room length on the right side; work your way to the left. Raise drum. Start motor. Slowly lower drum to floor. Lift the sander off the floor when you reach the wall. Move to the left 2 to 4" and then walk it backwards the same distance you just walked forward. Repeat.

Sandpapers for Drum Sanders & Edgers ▸

Grits	Grade	Use
20, 30, 40, 60	Coarse	To level uneven boards
100, 120	Medium	To minimize scratches from coarse grits
150, 180	Fine	To eliminate scratches from medium grits

Sandpaper becomes less effective over time; it may even rip. Buy 3–5 sheets of every grade for each room you want to refinish. You won't use them all, but most rentals allow you to return what you don't use. It's far better to have too many than to find yourself unable to continue until the next day because you ran out and the hardware store is closed.

Reminder: before you leave the rental shop, have an employee show you how to load the paper. Every machine is a little different.

(continued)

4

When you get to the far left side of the room, turn the machine around and repeat the process. Overlap the sanded section two-thirds to feather out the ridgeline. Repeat the sanding process 3 or 4 more times using 120-grit sandpaper. Sand the entire floor. For the final passes, use finer sandpaper (150- to 180-grit) to remove scratches left by coarser papers.

5

Power edge sander

To sand hard-to-reach spots, first use a power edge sander along the walls, using the same grit that you last used with the drum sander. Make a succession of overlapping half-circles starting in the corner on one wall. Pull out in an arc and then swirl back to the wall. Continue around the room. Blend together any lines left by the drum and edge sanders by running a rotary buffer over the floor twice: first with an 80-grit screen and then with a 100-grit screen. Finally, use a 5" random orbital sander to smooth out the floor. The random motion naturally feathers out bumps.

6

Use a paint scraper to get to corners and hard-to-reach nooks and crannies. Pull the scraper toward you with a steady downward pressure. Pull with the grain. Next, sand with a sanding block.

7

Prepare the room for finish by sweeping and vacuuming. Remove plastic on the doors, windows, and fixtures. Sweep and vacuum again. Wipe up fine particles with a tack cloth.

Apply polyurethane finish. Mix equal parts water-based polyurethane and water. Use a natural bristle brush to apply the mixture along walls and around obstacles. To apply the mixture in the middle of the room, use a painting pad on a pole. Apply 2 coats diagonally across the grain and a final coat in the direction of the grain.

Allow the finish to dry after each coat. Lightly buff the floor with a fine to medium abrasive pad. Clean the floor with a damp cloth and wipe the area dry with a towel.

Apply at least two coats of undiluted polyurethane finish to get a hard, durable finish. Allow the finish to dry; repeat step 9 and then add a final coat. Do not overbrush.

After the final coat is dry, buff the surface with water and a fine abrasive pad. This removes surface imperfections and diminishes gloss. After finishing, wait at least 72 hours before replacing the shoe molding.

Repairs

Floor coverings wear out faster than other interior surfaces, and surface damage can affect more than just appearance. Scratches in resilient flooring and cracks in grouted tile joints can let moisture into the floor's underpinnings. Hardwood floors lose their finish and can become permanently discolored. Loose boards squeak.

Moisture underneath finished flooring can ruin wood underlayment and eventually the subfloor. Bathroom floors suffer the most from moisture problems. Subflooring can pull loose from joists, causing floors to become uneven and springy.

You can fix problems like this yourself, including squeaks, damaged baseboards and trim, and minor damage to floor coverings, with the tools and techniques shown on the following pages.

In this chapter:

- Fixing Squeaky Floors
- Replacing Trim Moldings
- Repairing Hardwood
- Replacing Laminate Planks
- Repairing Resilient Flooring
- Repairing Carpet
- Repairing Tile

Fixing Squeaky Floors

Floors squeak when floorboards rub against each other or against the nails securing them to the subfloor or if they haven't been nailed properly. Normal changes in wood make some squeaking inevitable, although noisy floors can indicate serious structural problems. If an area of a floor is soft or excessively squeaky, inspect the framing and the foundation supporting the floor.

Whenever possible, fix squeaks from underneath the floor. Joists longer than eight feet should have X-bridging or solid blocking between each pair to help distribute the weight. If these supports aren't present, install them every six feet to stiffen and help silence a noisy floor.

To pinpoint the source of a squeak, have someone walk around upstairs while you're below the floor (on the lower level). Make a pencil mark on the unfinished ceiling where you hear the offending chirp or squawk. The subfloor may even visually move away from the joists when you hear the squeak. If you don't see any movement, the finished flooring has buckled up away from the subfloor. If this is the case, have the person upstairs place a heavy weight, such as a couch leg or cinder block, on the spot that squeaks. If the squeak is immediately over a joist, use a hammer to tap a wood shim between the joist and subfloor.

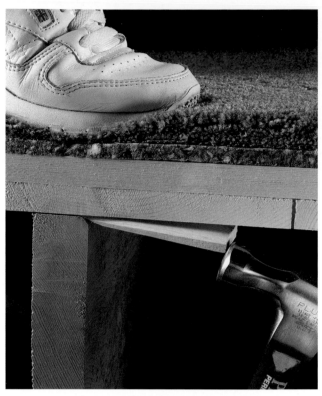

Gaps between the subfloor and the floor joists are leading causes of squeaky floors. If you have access from below, finding the gap and driving in a wood shim can eliminate the audible rubbing.

Fixes for Squeaky Floors

If you can access floor joists from underneath, drive wood screws up through the subfloor to draw hardwood flooring and the subfloor together. Drill pilot holes and make certain the screws aren't too long, causing them to break through the floorboards. Determine the combined thickness of the floor and subfloor by measuring at cutouts for pipes.

Install wood bridging if your joists appear to be shifting or moving—this lack of rigidity can cause squeaking and bouncing as you walk on the floor. You can use 2 × 4 lumber with the ends beveled to match the angle of the joists when installed diagonally, or you can buy metal bridging at any building center.

How to Make & Use a Beater Block

Make a "beater" block. If loose nails are the problem, you can tap the floorboards down where you hear the squeak. Wrap a 2 × 4 scrap (length of 1 ft. should do) in a scrap of carpet so that you don't scratch the floor surface. Tack the carpet to the top of the 2 × 4 with nails.

Place the 2 × 4 at a right angle to the squeaky floorboards. Tap the 2 × 4 with a hammer to reseat any loose boards or nails. Start at the perimeter of the squeaky section, moving the 2 × 4 in a rectangular pattern until you get to the center.

Preventing Squeaks

Because small squeaks can be caused by dirt between floorboards or by dryness, clean the floor at least once a week.

Squeaks in hardwood floors caused by floorboards rubbing against each other or against a nail can sometimes be eliminated for a few weeks or months just by adding a hardwood floor lubricant at the point of friction. First remove dirt and debris from between the floorboards using an old toothbrush. With a clean toothbrush or a clean cloth, apply the lubricant to the floor joints.

How to Install Anti-squeak Hardware

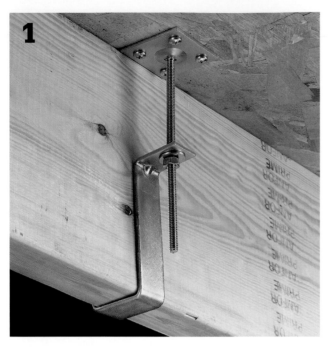

Squeak elimination hardware products are designed to draw the flooring subfloor and the floor joists together. This is a perfect solution for squeaks in floors with surfaces that you cannot drive a fastener through, such as ceramic tile. The product seen here consists of a mounting plate, a threaded rod, and a J-strap that cradles the underside of the joist.

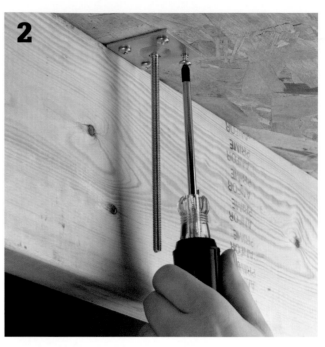

Insert the head of the hanger bolt into the concave part of the anchor plate. Use a Phillips screwdriver to screw the mounting plate to the underside of the subfloor (four screws are often provided). You want the plate to be touching the nearest joist in the general area of the squeak.

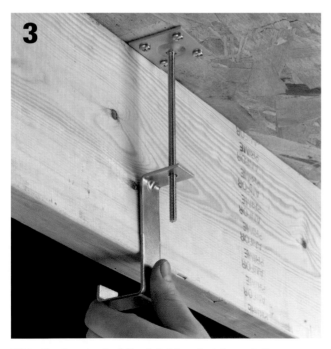

Slide the top part of the joist bracket through the threaded hanger rod and the bottom part under the joist.

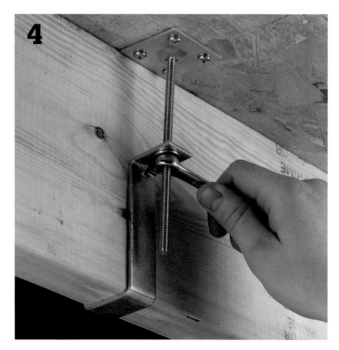

Slip the washer and hex nut onto the rod. With a wrench, tighten the nut until the subfloor is pulled snug against the joist. Avoid overtightening.

How to Fasten Loose Floorboards

The surest way to reattach loose or buckled floorboards is from above. Start by drilling pilot holes for several flooring nails in the floorboard only. The nail will grip better if you do not predrill the wood underlayment and subfloor.

Use a hammer and nail set to drive the flooring nail heads well below the surface of the flooring. The goal is to create enough space above the nail head for wood filler to take hold and stick.

Fill the nail holes with wood putty. The best match is usually obtained with pretinted wood putty, as opposed to untinted wood putty that is intended to be stained to match after it dries. Press the putty to make sure it gets all the way into the nailhole, and overfill slightly.

Sand the dried wood putty so it is flat and flush with the surrounding wood surface. Use fine grit sandpaper (180 or 220 grit) and avoid disturbing the surrounding wood finish as much as you can. Once you have smoothed the patch, wipe it clean with a dry cloth and then dab clear polyurethane varnish over the patch, feathering it lightly onto the surrounding surface, to protect the patch and darken it slightly (inset).

Replacing Trim Moldings

There's no reason to let damaged trim moldings detract from the appearance of a well-maintained room. With the right tools and a little attention to detail, you can replace or repair them quickly and easily.

Home centers and lumberyards sell many styles of moldings, but they may not stock moldings found in older homes. If you have trouble finding duplicates, check salvage yards in your area. They sometimes carry styles no longer manufactured. You can also try combining several different moldings to duplicate a more elaborate version.

Tools & Materials ▸

Flat pry bars (2)	Nail set
Coping saw	Wood scraps
Miter saw	Replacement moldings
Drill	2d, 4d, and 6d finish nails
Hammer	Wood putty

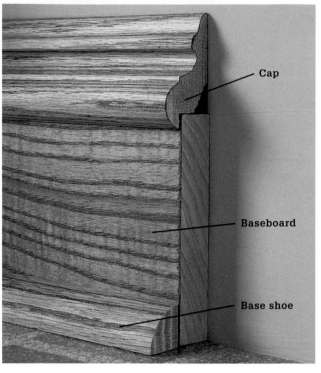

If you can't find your exact trim molding at a local lumberyard, try recreating it with multiple pieces.

How to Remove Damaged Trim

1

Even the lightest pressure from a pry bar can damage wallboard or plaster, so use a large, flat scrap of wood to protect the wall. Insert one bar beneath the trim and work the other bar between the baseboard and the wall. Force the pry bars in opposite directions to remove the baseboard.

2

To remove baseboards without damaging the wall, use leverage rather than force. Pry off the base shoe first using a flat pry bar. When you feel a few nails pop, move farther along the molding and pry again.

How to Install Baseboards

1

Start at an inside corner by butting one piece of baseboard securely into the corner. Drill pilot holes, then fasten the baseboard with two 6d finish nails, aligned vertically, at each wall stud. Cut a scrap of baseboard so the ends are perfectly square. Cut the end of the workpiece square. Position the scrap on the back of the workpiece so its back face is flush with the end of the workpiece. Trace the outline of the scrap onto the back of the workpiece.

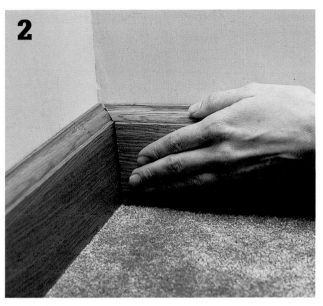

2

Cut along the outline on the workpiece with a coping saw, keeping the saw perpendicular to the baseboard face. Test-fit the coped end. Recut it, if necessary.

3

To cut the baseboard to fit at outside corners, mark the end where it meets the outside wall corner. Cut the end at a 45° angle using a power miter saw. Locknail all miter joints by drilling a pilot hole and driving 4d finish nails through each corner.

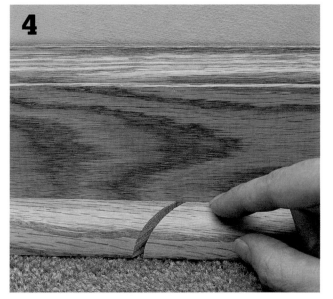

4

Install base shoe molding along the bottom of the baseboards. Make miter joints at inside and outside corners, and fasten base shoe with 2d finish nails. Whenever possible, complete a run of molding using one piece. For long spans, join molding pieces by mitering the ends at parallel 45° angles. Set nail heads below the surface using a nail set, and then fill the holes with wood putty.

Repairing Hardwood

A darkened, dingy hardwood floor may only need a thorough cleaning to reveal an attractive, healthy finish. If you have a fairly new or prefinished hardwood floor, check with the manufacturer or flooring installer before applying any cleaning products or wax. Most prefinished hardwood, for example, should not be waxed.

Water and other liquids can penetrate deep into the grain of older hardwood floors, leaving dark stains that are sometimes impossible to remove by sanding. Instead, try bleaching the wood with oxalic acid, available in crystal form at home centers or paint stores. When gouges, scratches, and dents aren't bad enough to warrant replacing a floorboard, repair the damaged area with a latex wood patch that matches the color of your floor.

Identify surface finishes using solvents. In an inconspicuous area, rub in different solvents to see if the finish dissolves, softens, or is removed. Denatured alcohol removes shellac, while lacquer thinner removes lacquer. If neither of those work, try nail polish remover containing acetone, which removes varnish but not polyurethane.

Tools & Materials ▸

Vacuum	Cloths	Wood restorer	Scrubbing brush or
Buffing machine	Hardwood cleaning kit	Latex wood patch	nylon scrubbing pad
Hammer	Paste wax	Sandpaper	Disposable cup
Nail set	Rubber gloves	Dishwashing detergent	Borax
Putty knife	Oxalic acid		

How to Clean & Renew Hardwood

Vacuum the entire floor. Mix hot water and dishwashing detergent that doesn't contain lye, trisodium phosphate, or ammonia. Working on 3-ft.-square sections, scrub the floor with a brush or nylon scrubbing pad. Wipe up the water and wax with a towel before moving to the next section.

If the water and detergent don't remove the old wax, use a hardwood floor cleaning kit. Use only solvent-type cleaners, as some water-based products can blacken wood. Apply the cleaner following the manufacturer's instructions.

When the floor is clean and dry, apply a high-quality floor wax. Paste wax is more difficult to apply than liquid floor wax, but it lasts much longer. Apply the wax by hand, then polish the floor with a rented buffing machine fitted with synthetic buffing pads.

How to Remove Stains

Remove the finish by sanding the stained area. In a disposable cup, dissolve the recommended amount of oxalic acid crystals in water. Wearing rubber gloves, pour the mixture over the stained area, taking care to cover only the darkened wood.

Let the liquid stand for one hour. Repeat the application, if necessary. Wash with 2 tablespoons borax dissolved in one pint water to neutralize the acid. Rinse with water, and let the wood dry. Sand the area smooth.

Apply several coats of wood restorer until the bleached area matches the finish of the surrounding floor.

How to Patch Scratches & Small Holes

Before filling nail holes, make sure the nails are securely set in the wood. Use a hammer and nail set to drive loose nails below the surface. Apply wood patch to the damaged area using a putty knife. Force the compound into the hole by pressing the knife blade downward until it lies flat on the floor.

Scrape excess compound from the edges, and allow the patch to dry completely. Sand the patch flush with the surrounding surface. Using fine-grit sandpaper, sand in the direction of the wood grain.

Apply wood restorer to the sanded area until it blends with the rest of the floor.

Replacing Damaged Floorboards

As durable and renewable as wood floors are, they are sometimes damaged beyond what simple refinishing can fix. A deep scratch or scar that extends down further than the surface of the board can't be sanded out without making a noticeable dip in the floor. In cases like this, it's time to remove the damaged wood entirely.

Whenever possible, it's best to replace entire boards. Where the strip is long or you simply want to make a more confined repair, you'll simple chisel out the section of the board with the damage, and replace it with a new piece (a good argument for the wise practice of keeping a couple extra strips in storage when installing a new floor).

Tools & Materials ▸

Carpenter's square	Wood chisel	Scrap wood	8d finish nails
Ruler	Small pry bar	Nail set	Cleaning tools
Painter's tape	Circular saw	Replacement planks	Sandpaper
Drill with spade bit	Mallet	Wood putty	Finishing materials
Hammer	Nails	Putty knife	

Replacing a small section of flooring boils down to finding a matching piece, trimming off the protruding tongue-and-groove parts and fastening it into the floor surface pattern.

How to Replace a Section of Wood Strip Flooring

Use a straightedge to draw cut lines above and below the damaged portion of the board. To avoid nails, be sure to mark cut lines at least ¾" inside the outermost edge of any joints. The goal is not to cut out the entire section of floorboard, but to remove a strip down the middle so you can create room to pry it out.

Determine the depth of the boards to be cut. With a drill and ¾"-wide spade bit, slowly drill through a damaged board. Drill until you see the top of the subfloor. Measure the depth. A common depth is ⅝ or ¾". Set your circular saw to this depth.

To prevent boards from chipping, place painter's tape along the outside of the pencil lines. To create a wood cutting guide, tack a straight wood strip inside the damaged area (for easy removal, allow nails to slightly stick up). Set the guide back the distance between the saw blade and the guide edge of the circular saw.

Align the circular saw with the wood cutting guide. Turn on the saw. Lower the blade into the cutline. Do not cut the last ¼" of the corners. Remove cutting guide. Repeat with other sides.

(continued)

5

Complete the cuts. Use a hammer and sharp chisel to completely loosen the boards from the subfloor. Make sure the chisel's beveled side is facing the damaged area for a clean edge.

6

Remove split boards. Use a scrap 2 × 4 block for leverage and to protect the floor. With a hammer, tap a pry bar into and under the split board. Most boards pop out easily, but some may require a little pressure. Remove exposed nails with the hammer claw.

7

Use a chisel to remove the 2 remaining strips. Again, make sure the bevel side of the chisel is facing the interior of the damaged area. Set any exposed nails with your nail set.

Trimming Tongues & Grooves ▸

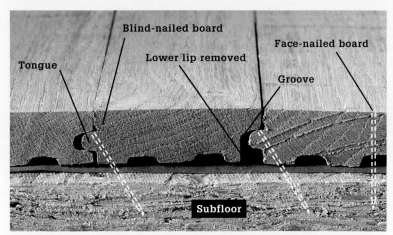

Blind-nailed board

Lower lip removed

Face-nailed board

Tongue

Groove

Subfloor

When tongue-and-groove hardwood floors are installed, each new course is blind-nailed through the tongue before the next course is placed. The process is called "blind-nailing" because you can't see the nail after the floor is finished because it is angled into the tongue-and-groove joint. This brings up two points: 1. You should be aware of the nails angled into the groove side of every board, so you have a better chance of avoiding them when you are cutting or drilling into floorboards. 2. The last board you install has to be "facenailed" (nailed through the top of the board) because you no longer have access to the tongue. The lower lip of this board is first removed, to fit into place.

8

Cut strips of new flooring to the length and width and slip the patch strip into the repair opening, forming the tongue-and-groove joint with the board at the edge of the opening. If you are installing a single board, trim off the bottom shoulder of the groove edge first (see tip, previous page).

9

To install the last board, hook the tongue into the groove of the old floor and then use a soft mallet to tap the groove side down into the previous board installed.

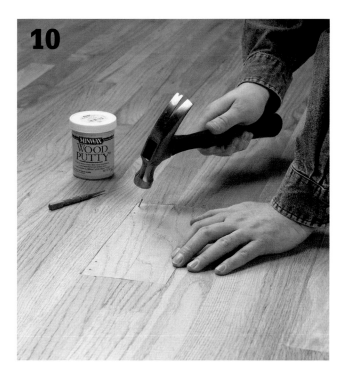

10

Drill pilot holes angled outward: two side-by-side holes about ½" from the edges of each board, and one hole every 12" along the groove side of each board. Drive 1½"-long, 8d finish nails through the holes. Set nails with a nail set. Fill holes with wood putty.

11

Once putty is dry, sand the patch smooth with fine-grit sandpaper. Feather sand neighboring boards. Vacuum and wipe the area with a clean cloth. Apply matching wood stain or restorer; then apply 2 coats of matching finish. To find out what type of finish your floor has, see page 242.

Replacing Laminate Planks

In the event that you need to replace a laminate plank, you must first determine how to remove the damaged plank. If you have a glueless "floating" floor it is best to unsnap and remove each plank starting at the wall and moving in until you reach the damaged plank. However, if the damaged plank is far from the wall it is more time-efficient to cut out the damaged plank.

Fully-bonded laminate planks have adhesive all along the bottom of the plank and are secured directly to the underlayment. When you remove the damaged plank, you run the risk of gouging the subfloor, so we recommend calling in a professional if you find that your laminate planks are completely glued to the subfloor.

As indestructible as laminate floors may seem, scratches caused by normal day-to-day wear and tear are unavoidable. Whether the damaged plank is close to a wall or in the middle of the floor, this project will show you how to replace it.

Tools & Materials ▸

Chisel	Vacuum
Hammer	Eye and ear protection
Flat pry bar	Scrap plywood and 2 × 4
Wood shims	Pliers
Replacement plank	Clamps
Nail set	Router
Finish nails	Sandpaper
Wood putty	Suction cup
Drill	Laminate glue
Straightedge	Wax paper
Painter's tape	Towel
Circular saw	Weights

Cross-section of a Laminate Plank ▸

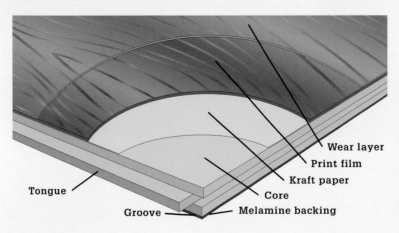

Tongue

Groove — — Melamine backing

Core

Kraft paper

Print film

Wear layer

From bottom to top, laminate planks are engineered to resist moisture, scratches, and dents. A melamine base layer protects the inner core layer, which is most often HDF (high-density fiberboard). This is occasionally followed by kraft paper saturated in resins for added protection and durability. The print film is a photographic layer that replicates the look of wood or ceramic. The surface is a highly protective wear layer. The tongue-and-groove planks fit together tightly and may be (according to manufacturer's instructions) glued together for added stability.

How to Replace a Damaged Plank

To remove shoe molding, wedge a chisel between the shoe molding and baseboards to create a gap and maintain that gap with wood shims. Continue this process every 6" along the wall. Locate the nails that are holding the shoe to the baseboard and use a pry bar at those locations to gently pull the shoe away from the baseboard (inset).

To remove the first plank closest to the wall, use a pry bar to lift it just enough to get your hands under it and then slowly lift up and away from the adjacent plank. Continue to remove the planks that are between the shoe molding and the damaged plank with your hands. Finally, remove the damaged plank.

Snap in a new replacement plank and then continue to replace the rest of the boards until you reach the wall in the same manner.

Lay the shoe molding back in place along the wall. Using a nail set and hammer, countersink finish nails into the top of the shoe molding every 6 to 12" along the wall. Fill the holes with wood putty.

How to Replace a Damaged Plank in the Center of the Floor

Draw a rectangle in the middle of the damaged board with a 1½" border between the rectangle and factory edges. At each rectangle corner and inside each corner of the plank, use a hammer and nail set to make indentations. At each of these indentations, drill ³⁄₁₆" holes into the plank. Only drill the depth of the plank.

To protect the floor from chipping, place painter's tape along the cutlines. Now, set the circular saw depth to the thickness of the replacement plank. (If you don't have a replacement plank, see page 245, step 2 to determine the plank thickness.) To plunge cut the damaged plank, turn on the saw and slowly lower the blade into the cutline until the cut guide rests flat on the floor. Push the saw from the center of the line out to each end. Stop ¼" from each corner. Place a sharp chisel between the two drill holes in each corner and strike with a hammer to complete each corner cut. Lift and remove the middle section. Vacuum.

To remove the remaining outer edges of the damaged plank, place a scrap 2 × 4 wood block along the outside of one long cut and use it for leverage to push a pry bar under the flooring. Insert a second pry bar beneath the existing floor (directly under the joint of the adjacent plank) and use a pliers to grab the 1½" border strip in front of the pry bar. Press downward until a gap appears at the joint. Remove the border piece. Remove the opposite strip and the two short end pieces in the same manner.

Place a scrap of cardboard in the opening to protect the underlayment while you remove all of the old glue from the factory edges with a chisel. Vacuum up the wood and glue flakes.

Replacing Laminate Planks

In the event that you need to replace a laminate plank, you must first determine how to remove the damaged plank. If you have a glueless "floating" floor it is best to unsnap and remove each plank starting at the wall and moving in until you reach the damaged plank. However, if the damaged plank is far from the wall it is more time-efficient to cut out the damaged plank.

Fully-bonded laminate planks have adhesive all along the bottom of the plank and are secured directly to the underlayment. When you remove the damaged plank, you run the risk of gouging the subfloor, so we recommend calling in a professional if you find that your laminate planks are completely glued to the subfloor.

As indestructible as laminate floors may seem, scratches caused by normal day-to-day wear and tear are unavoidable. Whether the damaged plank is close to a wall or in the middle of the floor, this project will show you how to replace it.

Tools & Materials ▸

Chisel	Vacuum
Hammer	Eye and ear protection
Flat pry bar	Scrap plywood and 2 × 4
Wood shims	Pliers
Replacement plank	Clamps
Nail set	Router
Finish nails	Sandpaper
Wood putty	Suction cup
Drill	Laminate glue
Straightedge	Wax paper
Painter's tape	Towel
Circular saw	Weights

Cross-section of a Laminate Plank ▸

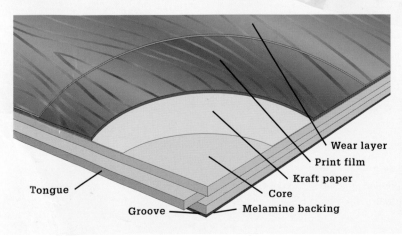

Tongue
Groove
Wear layer
Print film
Kraft paper
Core
Melamine backing

From bottom to top, laminate planks are engineered to resist moisture, scratches, and dents. A melamine base layer protects the inner core layer, which is most often HDF (high-density fiberboard). This is occasionally followed by kraft paper saturated in resins for added protection and durability. The print film is a photographic layer that replicates the look of wood or ceramic. The surface is a highly protective wear layer. The tongue-and-groove planks fit together tightly and may be (according to manufacturer's instructions) glued together for added stability.

Cut strips of new flooring to the length and width and slip the patch strip into the repair opening, forming the tongue-and-groove joint with the board at the edge of the opening. If you are installing a single board, trim off the bottom shoulder of the groove edge first (see tip, previous page).

To install the last board, hook the tongue into the groove of the old floor and then use a soft mallet to tap the groove side down into the previous board installed.

Drill pilot holes angled outward: two side-by-side holes about ½" from the edges of each board, and one hole every 12" along the groove side of each board. Drive 1½"-long, 8d finish nails through the holes. Set nails with a nail set. Fill holes with wood putty.

Once putty is dry, sand the patch smooth with fine-grit sandpaper. Feather sand neighboring boards. Vacuum and wipe the area with a clean cloth. Apply matching wood stain or restorer; then apply 2 coats of matching finish. To find out what type of finish your floor has, see page 242.

5

To remove the tongues on one long and one short end, lay the replacement plank face down onto a protective scrap of plywood (or 2 × 4). Clamp a straight cutting guide to the replacement plank so the distance from the guide causes the bit to align with the tongue and trim it off. Pressing the router against the cutting guide, slowly move along the entire edge of the replacement plank to remove the tongue. Clean the edges with sandpaper.

6

Dry-fit the grooves on the replacement board into the tongues of the surrounding boards and press into place. If the board fits snugly between the surrounding boards, pry the plank up with a manufacturer suction cup. If the plank does not sit flush with the rest of the floor, check to make sure you routered the edges off evenly. Sand any rough edges that should have been completely removed and try to fit the plank again.

7

Set the replacement plank by applying laminate glue to the removed edges of the replacement plank and into the grooves of the existing planks. Firmly press the plank into place.

8

Clean up glue with a damp towel. Place a strip of wax paper over the new plank and evenly distribute some books on the wax paper. Allow the adhesive to dry for 12 to 24 hours.

Repairing Resilient Flooring

Repair methods for resilient sheet flooring depend on the type of floor as well as the type of damage. With sheet vinyl, you can fuse the surface or patch in new material. With linoleum, a patch is usually the only way to repair serious damage.

Small cuts and scratches can be fused permanently and nearly invisibly with liquid seam sealer, a clear compound that's available wherever vinyl flooring is sold. For tears or burns, the damaged area can be patched. If necessary, remove vinyl from a hidden area, such as under an appliance, to use as patch material. Linoleum scratches and small damage can be repaired with a paste made from wood glue and shavings of scrap linoleum.

When sheet flooring is badly worn, or the damage is widespread, the only answer is complete replacement. Although it's possible to add layers of flooring in some situations, evaluate the options carefully. Be aware that the backing of older vinyl tiles made of asphalt may contain asbestos fibers.

Tools & Materials ▸

Carpenter's square	Plywood scrap
Utility knife	Duct tape
Putty knife	Chisel
Heat gun	Flooring scraper
J-roller	Cloth
Notched trowel	Lacquer thinner
Masking tape	Applicator bottle
Scrap of	Weights
matching flooring	
Mineral spirits	
Floor covering	
adhesive	
Wax paper	
Liquid seam sealer	
Tape measure	

When sheet flooring is damaged, the best remedy is to slice out the damaged area and replace it with new material, carefully seaming the edges of the patch.

How to Patch Sheet Vinyl

Measure the width and length of the damaged area. Place the new flooring remnant on a surface you don't mind making some cuts on—like a scrap of plywood. Use a carpenter's square for a cutting guide. Make sure your cutting size is a bit larger than the damaged area.

Lay the patch over the damaged area, matching pattern lines. Secure the patch with duct tape. Using a carpenter's square as a cutting guide, cut through the new vinyl (on top) and the old vinyl (on bottom). Press firmly with the knife to cut both layers.

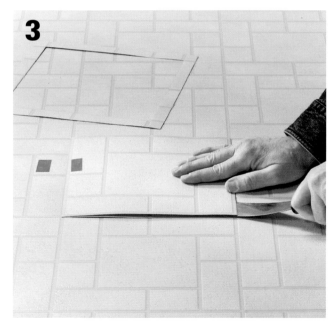

Use tape to mark one edge of the new patch with the corresponding edge of the old flooring as placement marks. Remove the tape around the perimeter of the patch and lift up.

Soften the underlying adhesive with an electric heat gun and remove the damaged section of floor. Work from edges in. When the tile is loosened, insert a putty knife and pry up the damaged area.

(continued)

Scrape off the remaining adhesive with a putty knife or chisel. Work from the edges to the center. Dab mineral spirits or spritz warm water on the floor to dissolve leftover goop, taking care not to use too much; you don't want to loosen the surrounding flooring. Use a razor-edged scraper (flooring scraper) to scrape to the bare wood underlayment.

Apply adhesive to the patch using a notched trowel (with ⅛" V-shaped notches) held at a 45° angle to the back of the new vinyl patch.

Set one edge of the patch in place. Lower the patch onto the underlayment. Press into place. Apply pressure with a J-roller or rolling pin to create a solid bond. Start at the center and work toward the edges, working out air bubbles. Wipe up adhesive that oozes out the sides with a clean, damp cloth or sponge.

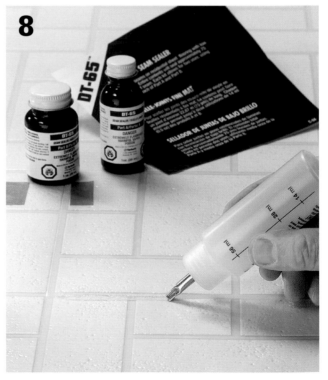

Let the adhesive dry overnight. Use a soft cloth dipped in lacquer thinner to clean the area. Mix the seam sealer according to the manufacturer's directions. Use an applicator bottle to apply a thin bead of sealer onto the cutlines.

How to Replace Resilient Tile

Use an electric heat gun to warm the damaged tile and soften the underlying adhesive. Keep the heat source moving so you don't melt the tile. When an edge of the tile begins to curl, insert a putty knife to pry up the loose edge until you can remove the tile. *Note: If you can clearly see the seam between tiles, first score around the tile with a utility knife. This prevents other tiles from lifting.*

Scrape away remaining adhesive with a putty knife or, for stubborn spots, a floor scraper. Work from the edges to the center so that you don't accidentally scrape up the adjacent tiles. Use mineral spirits to dissolve leftover goop. Take care not to allow the mineral spirits to soak into the floor under adjacent tiles. Vacuum up dust, dirt, and adhesive. Wipe clean.

When the floor is dry, use a notched trowel—with ⅛" V-shaped notches—held at a 45° angle to apply a thin, even layer of vinyl tile adhesive onto the underlayment. *Note: Only follow this step if you have dry-back tiles.*

Set one edge of the tile in place. Lower the tile onto the underlayment and then press it into place. Apply pressure with a J-roller to create a solid bond, starting at the center and working toward the edge to work out air bubbles. If adhesive oozes out the sides, wipe it up with a damp cloth or sponge. Cover the tile with wax paper and some books, and let the adhesive dry for 24 hours.

Repairing Carpet

Burns and stains are the most common carpeting problems. You can clip away the burned fibers of superficial burns using small scissors. Deeper burns and indelible stains require patching by cutting away and replacing the damaged area.

Another common problem, addressed on the opposite page, is carpet seams or edges that have come loose. You can rent the tools necessary for fixing this problem.

Tools & Materials ▸

Cookie-cutter tool
Knee kicker
4" wallboard knife
Utility knife
Seam iron
Seam adhesive

Replacement carpeting
Double-face carpet tape
Heat-activated seam tape
Weights
Boards

Stained or damaged carpet can be replaced with specialized tools and DIY techniques.

How to Repair Spot Damage

Use a cookie-cutter tool to cut a replacement patch from scrap carpeting. Press the cutter down over the damaged area and twist it to cut away the carpet.

Remove extensive damage or stains with the cookie-cutter tool (available at carpeting stores). Insert double-face carpet tape under the cutout, positioning the tape so it overlaps the patch seams.

Press the patch into place. Make sure the direction of the nap or pattern matches the existing carpet. To seal the seam and prevent unraveling, apply seam adhesive to the edges of the patch.

How to Restretch Loose Carpet

Adjust the knob on the head of the knee kicker so the prongs grab the carpet backing without penetrating through the padding. Starting from a corner or near a point where the carpet is firmly attached, press the knee kicker head into the carpet, about 2" from the wall.

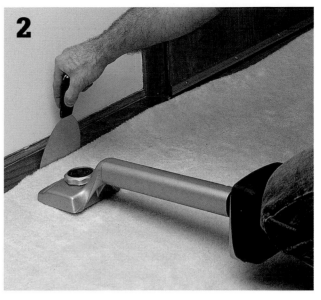

Thrust your knee into the cushion of the knee kicker to force the carpet toward the wall. Tuck the carpet edge into the space between the wood strip and the baseboard using a 4" wallboard knife. If the carpet is still loose, trim the edge with a utility knife and stretch it again.

How to Glue Loose Seams

Remove the old tape from under the carpet seam. Cut a strip of new seam tape and place it under the carpet so it's centered along the seam with the adhesive facing up. Plug in the seam iron and let it heat up.

Pull up both edges of the carpet and set the hot iron squarely onto the tape. Wait about 30 seconds for the glue to melt. Move the iron about 12" farther along the seam. Quickly press the edges of the carpet together into the melted glue behind the iron. Separate the pile to make sure no fibers are stuck in the glue and the seam is tight. Place weighted boards over the seam to keep it flat while the glue sets. Remember, you have only 30 seconds to repeat the process.

Repairing Tile

Although ceramic tile is one of the hardest floor coverings, tiles sometimes become damaged and need to be replaced. Major cracks in grout joints indicate that floor movement has caused the adhesive layer beneath the tile to deteriorate. The adhesive layer must be replaced in order to create a permanent repair.

Any time you remove tile, check the underlayment. If it's no longer smooth, solid, and level, repair or replace it before replacing the tile. When removing grout or damaged tiles, be careful not to damage surrounding tiles. Always wear eye protection when working with a hammer and chisel.

Tools & Materials ▶

Hammer	Screwdriver	Grout	Cleaning tools
Cold chisel	Floor-leveling compound	Grout sealer	Nail set
Putty knife	Grout float	Grout sponge	Sandpaper
Square-notched trowel	Thin-set mortar	Grout saw	Scrap of wood
Rubber mallet	Replacement tile	Vacuum	Old toothbrush
Torpedo level	Scrap carpet or towel	Vinegar	Eye protection
Needlenose pliers	Tile spacers		

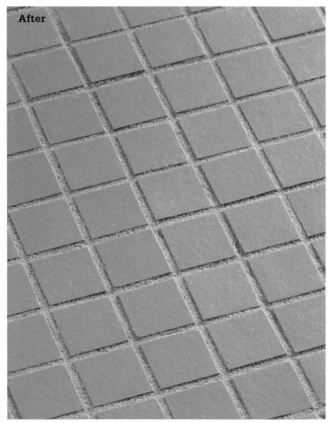

Tile repair should be done as soon as damage is observed. Whether the floor is made up of large floor tiles or smaller mosaics, once water and moisture get underneath a tile or two the damage spreads rapidly. Replace tiles as necessary, and regrout once old grout begins to discolor or crumble.

How to Regrout Tile

Scrape out the old grout with a grout saw or other tool, being careful not to scratch the tile faces or chip the edges. You may choose to regrout only the filed grout lines for a quick fix, but for more pleasing results and to prevent color variation in the grout lines, remove the grout around all tiles and regrout the entire floor.

Wash the tiled floor with a 1:1 mix of white vinegar and water, paying special attention to the areas around the tile joints. Vacuum the floor first to get rid of all debris.

Apply new grout. Prepare sanded grout mix according to the instructions on the package and then pack fresh grout deep into the joints using a rubber grout float. Hold the float at a 30° angle to the tiled surface.

Wipe diagonally across the tiles and grouted joints to remove excess grout and smooth the joints. Seal the grout joints with grout sealer after they've dried for a week or so. *Note: Sealing all the grout joints will help new grout lines blend with old grout if you're only doing a partial regrouting.*

How to Replace a Floor Tile

With a carbide-tipped grout saw, apply firm but gentle pressure across the grout until you expose the unglazed edges of the tile. Do not scratch the glazed tile surface. If the grout is stubborn, use a hammer and screwdriver to first tap the tile (step 2).

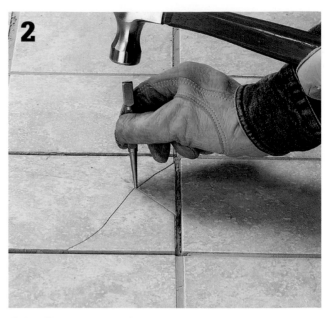

If the tile is not already cracked, use a hammer to puncture the tile by tapping a nail set or center punch into it. Alternatively, if the tile is significantly cracked, use a chisel to pry up the tile.

Insert a chisel into one of the cracks and gently tap the tile. Start at the center and chip outward so you don't damage the adjacent tiles. Be aware that cement board looks a lot like mortar when you're chiseling. Remove and discard the broken pieces.

Use a putty knife to scrape away old thinset adhesive; use a chisel for poured mortar installation. If the underlayment is covered with metal lath, you won't be able to get the area smooth; just clean it out the best you can. Once the adhesive is scraped from the underlayment, smooth the rough areas with sandpaper. If there are gouges in the underlayment, fill them with epoxy-based thinset mortar (for cementboard) or a floor-leveling compound (for plywood). Allow the area to dry completely.

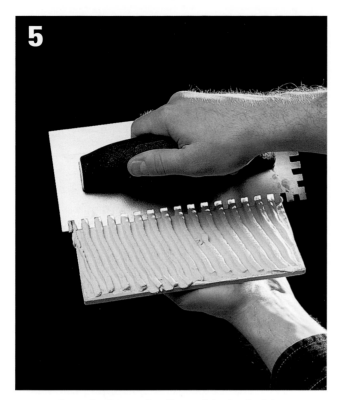

5

Use a ¼" notched trowel to "butter" the back of the replacement tile with thinset mortar. Set the tile down in position in the space, and press down until it is even with the adjacent tiles. Twist it a bit to get it to sit down in the mortar.

6

Use a rubber mallet to tap a block of scrap wood covered with cloth on top of the tile. Use a torpedo level to check that the tile is level with the surrounding tiles. Tap the tile until it's flush with the rest of the surrounding tiles. Use plastic spacers to ensure the tile is centered in the opening.

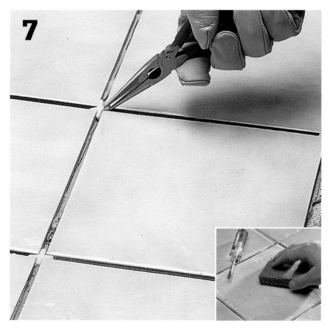

7

When the mortar has set, remove spacers with needlenose pliers. Remove mortar from grout joints with a small screwdriver and cloth, and then wipe away any mortar from the surface of the tile with a wet sponge. Let the area dry for at least 24 hours (or according to the manufacturer's recommendations).

8

Grout the joints with a putty knife. Fill in low spots by applying and smoothing extra grout with your fingertip. Use the round edge of a toothbrush handle to create a concave grout line, if desired.

DAMAGE	QUICK FIX
Minor scratches	Waxed floors—Apply a coat of wax (matching that already on the floor) and buff. Polyurethane floors—Touch-up kits are available at most home centers and hardware stores.
Food stains	Blot the stain with a damp cloth; if necessary, gently scrape food chunks off the floor with a plastic spatula.
Dark spots (ink, pet stains)	On a polyurethane-finished or wax-finished floor, remove the floor finish with #2 steel wool and then use a finish-specific wood cleaner or mineral spirits. Wash the area with household vinegar. If that doesn't work, lightly sand the area with fine sandpaper until the stain is gone; clean up dust with a tack cloth; stain, if required; and refinish with matching polyurethane or wax finish. The darker the stain, the deeper it is. To replace a floorboard, see page 240.
Oil and grease	Waxed floors—Soak up spilled oil or grease immediately. First blot the area with a dry cloth and then use a slightly damp cloth. If residue remains, wash the area with lye soap. Polyurethane floors—Apply mineral spirits or soap with trisodium phosphate (TSP) to a soft cloth and gently rub until the stain is gone.
Mold or mildew	Clean with an approved cleaner for your specific floor finish. On waxed floors, you may need to rub with #1 steel wool, then rewax and buff.
Surface damage	Damage such as water, burn marks, scratches, and gouges should be repaired immediately. Strip wax or oil finish by rubbing the floor with fine-grade steel wool or sandpaper. Once smooth, rewax or refinish.

As a last resort, stubborn sticky floors may need to be wet-mopped. Only wet mop the floor if the finish is in good condition. A sponge mop moistened with a mixture of water and a mild wood floor cleaner or a neutral pH soap or detergent (1 gal.: ½ cup cleaner) is all that is required. The mop should just barely be damp at any given time. Excess water can seriously damage wood floors. After cleaning, use a towel to thoroughly dry the floor.

Maintenance Tips: Concrete Floor ▸

DAMAGE	QUICK FIX
Grease and oil	Absorb with unscented cat litter. Sweep the oil-soaked litter onto newspaper. Throw the newspaper in a plastic bag and seal it. Dispose of this bag as hazardous waste. Scrub the area with hot liquid dish soap or laundry soap and water. Blot dry with towels and dispose of rags as hazardous waste. Alternatively, try commercial concrete degreaser.
Dark stains	Use diluted household bleach or dilute one cup of trisodium phosphate (TSP) in one gallon of hot water. Use a cloth soaked in the bleach to wipe the area clean.
Mold or mildew	Mix 1 part bleach with 3 parts warm water and let the mixture sit on the mildewed patch of floor until the mold lifts. Wipe the area clean with a dry towel.
Rust	Mix 1 part sodium citrate to 6 parts glycerin. Use a cloth to wash the area.
Copper, bronze, or ink	Mix 1 part ammonia to 9 parts water. Use a cloth to wash the area.
Iron	Mix 1 part oxalic acid to 9 parts water. Use a cloth to wash the area.
Latex paint	Use a scraper to loosen large chunks. Dip a stiff brush into soapy water and scrub.
Oil-based paint	Use a commercial paint remover or mineral spirits and a cloth to rub the area clean.

Caution! When working with acids or other strong cleaners, always wear long sleeves and pants, rubber gloves, and safety goggles and a mask or respirator that meets or surpasses the manufacturers recommendations. Make sure the work area is well ventilated.

Maintenance Tips: Ceramic Tile Floor ▸

DAMAGE	QUICK FIX
Discoloration	For grout joints, use oxygen bleach powder with water. Allow the solution to sit on the discolored area for at least 30 minutes. Gently scrub the area with a cloth or sponge. Rinse the floor with a damp mop. Allow the floor to dry.
Grease	Sponge or brush with water and household cleaner. Avoid ammonia products.
Blood, coffee, juice, wine, mustard	Make a paste of water and baking soda and apply it to the stain. If that doesn't do it, apply oxygen bleach and water. Allow the mixture to sit on the stained area for at least 30 minutes. Rinse with a damp mop. Rinse several times to remove the cleaning product, but do not get the floor too wet. Use a towel to dry the floor.
Latex paint	Gently scrape off what you can without scratching the tile. Scrub remaining paint with soap and water. Rinse thoroughly.
Oil-based paint	Use paint remover. If you use harsh chemicals on your tile, be sure to wash and rinse the area after cleaning. You may need to apply new sealer to the area as well.
Rust or mineral deposits	Use products specifically designed for removing these stains from the ceramic tiles.
Mildew or mold	Scrub the stain on white grout with an old toothbrush dipped in full-strength bleach (don't use with colored grout; use a commercial product instead).

Always check that products are specifically designed for your type of flooring before using generic household cleaners. Inappropriate cleaners can strip sealer from the floor. Also, always let your floor dry completely after following the cleaning steps above and then apply a sealer.

Caution! When working with acids or other strong cleaners, always wear long sleeves and pants, rubber gloves, and safety goggles and a mask or respirator that meets or surpasses the manufacturers recommendations. Make sure the work area is well ventilated.

Maintenance Tips: Resilient Floor ▶

DAMAGE	QUICK FIX
Wax	Carefully scrape the wax off the floor with a plastic scraper. If the wax is stubborn, follow the directions for wax in the chart for laminate floors, below.
Crayon	Dab a cloth in mineral spirits or the manufacturer's cleaner and scrub the area clean. Use a damp cloth to rinse the area after the crayon lifts.
Fruit juice, wine, mustard	Wipe the area with a cloth dabbed in full-strength bleach or a manufacturer's cleaner. If you use bleach, be sure to rinse until the surface is shining again.
Heel marks	Rub with a cloth dabbed in a nonabrasive cleaner.
Ink	Rub with a cloth dabbed in citrus-based cleaner or rubbing alcohol.
Nail polish	Rub with a cloth dabbed in acetone-based nail polish remover. Use a damp cloth to rinse the area.
Paint	While still wet, soak up paint with a dry cloth. Next, wipe the area with a cloth dabbed in mineral spirits. If dry, scrape the paint off with a plastic scraper and then wipe away the remaining paint with a cloth dabbed in rubbing alcohol.
Permanent marker	Rub the stain with a cloth dabbed in mineral spirits, nail polish remover, or rubbing alcohol. Use a damp cloth to rinse the area.
Rust	Mix 1 part oxalic acid to 10 parts water; carefully follow the acid manufacturer's directions, as this is an extremely caustic solution.
Shoe polish	Dab a cloth in a citrus-based cleaner or mineral spirits and rub the area.

Caution! Wear long sleeves, rubber gloves, goggles and a mask or respirator that meets or surpasses the manufacturers recommendations when working with acids or chemicals.

Maintenance Tips: Laminate Floor ▶

DAMAGE	QUICK FIX
Wax	Place a paper towel on the wax and lay an old towel over this. Set a warm clothing iron on the towel for a few seconds, just until the wax warms. Scrape the wax up with the plastic scraper or putty knife.
Crayon, heel marks	Rub with a dry cloth or a bit of acetone. Rinse the area with a damp cloth.
Fruit juice, wine	Rub with a dry cloth or a bit of commercial cleaner on a cloth. Rinse the area with a damp cloth.
Lipstick	Rub with a cloth just barely dabbed in acetone or paint thinner.
Nail polish	Dab a cloth in acetone-based nail polish remover and scrub the area; then rinse with a damp cloth.
Paint	While still wet, clean up latex paint with a damp cloth. If dry, scrape the paint off the floor with a plastic scraper.
Ink, tar, shoe polish	Scrub with a cloth dabbed in acetone or paint thinner. Rinse the area with a damp cloth.

Caution! Wear long sleeves, rubber gloves, goggles and a mask or respirator that meets or surpasses the manufacturers recommendations when working with strong chemicals.

Maintenance Tips: Carpet ▸

There may be more homegrown remedies for carpet spot removal than there are types of carpet. Perhaps the most ubiquitous of these remedies is club soda, alleged to cure stains from red wine to coffee and ketchup. This inexpensive carbonated drink mixer is known to lift stains to the surface so you can blot them up, while the salts help prevent staining. Whether you use home remedies or commercial products, always do a test in an inconspicuous area to make sure you don't bleach or stain your carpet.

Manufacturers have recommendations for cleaning products. Always check with your carpet manufacturer first, and adhere to their recommendations.

DAMAGE	QUICK FIX
Alcoholic beverages, candy, chocolate, eggs, fruit juice, gravy, ketchup, mustard, syrup, soft drinks, urine	Combine water, club soda, and vinegar—or use a carpet spot cleaner or shampoo. Depending on the type of carpet you have, follow the manufacturer's directions. Repeatedly blot the area to lift the stain. Allow the carpet to completely dry and then vacuum.
Butter, margarine, crayons, furniture polish, grease, motor oil, perfume, salad dressing, vegetable oil, shoe polish, tar	Apply a dry cleaner; if traces remain, apply a carpet shampoo product. Blot the stain with the cleaning product and then blot again with water to remove cleaning product residue. Allow the carpet to dry and then vacuum.
Blood, excrement, vomit	Sponge with cool water; add carpet shampoo and ammonia or white vinegar. Blot the area until the stain lifts. To remove cleaning residue, blot the area with water. Allow the carpet to dry and then vacuum.
Chewing gum	Chill the gum with ice cubes. With a dull knife, scrape off as much as possible. Blot area with a cloth and dry cleaner. Use a damp cloth to soak up the cleaning residue. Rinse the cloth frequently. Let dry. Vacuum.
Candle wax	Chill with ice cubes and scrape off as much as possible with a dull knife. Place paper towels and brown paper over the stain; iron on medium heat using a household iron to soak up wax. Apply dry cleaner, if necessary.
Nail polish	Wipe fresh spills with mild detergent and water. Don't use nail polish remover, it will dissolve polyester fibers. If the spill has set, try steam cleaning.
Burn marks	If only tips of the fiber are scorched, carefully scrape away the scorched portion using a fine, steel wool pad or razorblade.

Use a large spoon to pick up spills. Spoons capture liquids well without damaging fibers. Scoop toward the center of the stain to avoid spreading. Do not rub stains—blot them (see right). Apply cleaning solution to a cloth or paper towel, then blot the stain, working from the outside toward the center to avoid spreading the stain.

Resources

Black & Decker Corp.
Power tools & accessories
800-544-6986
www.blackanddecker.com

Cali Bamboo
Bamboo Flooring & Green Building Products
888-788-2254
www.calibamboo.com

Ceramic Tiles of Italy
www.italiatiles.com

Eco Friendly Flooring
866-250-3273
www.ecofriendlyflooring.com

Forbo Flooring Systems
Linoleum and linoleum tiles (Marmoleum®)
p. 122
www.forbo-flooring.com

HomerWood
Hardwood Floors
814-827-3855
www.homerwood.com

Koetter Woodworking
Kentucky Wood
812-923-8875
www.koetterwoodworking.com

LATICRETE
Floor warming mats & supplies
p. 80
800-243-4788
www.laticrete.com

Mirage
Prefinished Hardwood Floors
800-463-1303
www.miragefloors.com

Oceanside Glass Tile
Glass tile
p. 154
www.glasstile.com

Red Wing Shoes
Work boots and shoes shown throughout book
800-733-9464
www.redwingshoes.com

Room & Board
800-301-9720
www.roomandboard.com

SnapStone
Floating porcelain tile system
p. 160
877-263-5861
www.snapstone.com

Teragren Fine Bamboo Flooring, Panels & Veneer
Bamboo flooring
p. 102
800-929-6333
www.teragren.com

Photography Credits

Page 14, left / photo courtesy of HomerWood
Page 15, top left and bottom right / iStock photo
Page 15, top right and middle right/ Shutterstock
Page 16, left / Shutterstock
Page 17, left / Shutterstock
Page 18, both / Shutterstock
Page 19, top / Photolibrary
Page 19, bottom / photo courtesy of Forbo Flooring Systems
Page 21, top all / Shutterstock
Page 22, all / iStockphoto
Page 24 / iStockphoto
Page 25, top left / photo courtesy of MIRAGE Prefinished Hardwood Floors
Page 26, top / Shutterstock
Page 26, bottom / photo © Brand X Pictures/ Alamy
Page 27, top / photo courtesy of Ceramic Tiles of Italy
Page 27, bottom left / photo courtesy of Forbo Flooring Systems
Page 27, bottom right / Shutterstock
Page 28, top / photo courtesy of MIRAGE Prefinished Hardwood Floors
Page 28, bottom / photo courtesy of Marmoleum by Forbo Linoleum
Page 29, top / photo courtesy of Ceramic Tiles of Italy
Page 29, bottom / Red Cover/Alamy
Page 30, top / photo courtesy of Teragren
Page 30, bottom left / photo courtesy of Marmoleum

Page 30, bottom right / photo courtesy of Ceramic Tiles of Italy
Page 31, top / Shutterstock
Page 31, bottom / photo courtesy of Ceramic Tiles of Italy
Page 32, top / photo courtesy of Room and Board
Page 32, bottom / Shutterstock
Page 33, top / Red Cover/Alamy
Page 33, bottom / photo courtesy of Ceramic Tiles of Italy
Page 34, top / photo courtesy of Armstrong
Page 34, bottom left/ iStockphoto
Page 34, bottom right / Photolibrary
Page 35, top / photo courtesy of Cali Bamboo
Page 35, bottom / photo courtesy of Ceramic Tiles of Italy
Page 36, top / photo courtesy of Marmoleum
Page 36, bottom / photo courtesy of Ceramic tiles of Italy
Page 37, top / photo courtesy of Ceramic Tiles of Italy
Page 37, bottom / photo courtesy of HomerWood
Page 38, top / photo courtesy of Room and Board
Page 39, top / photo courtesy of Kohler
Page 39, bottom / iStockphoto
Page 40, top / photo courtesy of Room and Board
Page 40, bottom / photo courtesy of Ceramic Tiles of Italy
Page 41, top left / photo courtesy of Ceramic Tiles of Italy

Page 41, top right / Van Robaeys/Inside/ Beateworks
Page 41, bottom / photo courtesy of Teragren
Page 42, top / photo courtesy of Forbo Flooring Systems
Page 42, bottom / photo courtesy of Forbo Flooring Systems
Page 43, top left / photo courtesy of Ceramic Tiles of Italy
Page 43, top right / photo courtesy of Teragren
Page 43, bottom / photo courtesy of Ceramic Tiles of Italy
Page 44, top / photo courtesy of Teragren
Page 44, bottom / photo courtesy of Eco Friendly Flooring
Page 45, top / photo Benny Chan Photography, courtesy of Plyboo
Page 45, bottom / photo courtesy of Ceramic Tiles of Italy
Page 100, top / photo courtesy of Oshkosh Designs
Pages 103-107 / Bamboo courtesy of Teragren
Page 108 / photo courtesy of Kentucky Wood Floors
Page 122 / photo courtesy of Forbo Flooring Systems
Page 123 / photo courtesy of Forbo Flooring Systems
Page 126, left / photo courtesy of Armstrong
Pages 154-155 / photos © Oceanside Glass Tile
Page 172 / photo courtesy of BLTC
Page 174 / photo courtesy LivedIn Images
Page 185 / Shutterstock
Page 214 / photo courtesy of Armstrong

Conversion Charts

Lumber Dimensions

Nominal - U.S.	Actual - U.S. (in inches)	Metric	Nominal - U.S.	Actual - U.S. (in inches)	Metric
1 × 2	¾ × 1½	19 × 38 mm	1½ × 4	1¼ × 3½	32 × 89 mm
1 × 3	¾ × 2½	19 × 64 mm	1½ × 6	1¼ × 5½	32 × 140 mm
1 × 4	¾ × 3½	19 × 89 mm	1½ × 8	1¼ × 7¼	32 × 184 mm
1 × 5	¾ × 4½	19 × 114 mm	1½ × 10	1¼ × 9¼	32 × 235 mm
1 × 6	¾ × 5½	19 × 140 mm	1½ × 12	1¼ × 11¼	32 × 286 mm
1 × 7	¾ × 6¼	19 × 159 mm	2 × 4	1½ × 3½	38 × 89 mm
1 × 8	¾ × 7¼	19 × 184 mm	2 × 6	1½ × 5½	38 × 140 mm
1 × 10	¾ × 9¼	19 × 235 mm	2 × 8	1½ × 7¼	38 × 184 mm
1 × 12	¾ × 11¼	19 × 286 mm	2 × 10	1½ × 9¼	38 × 235 mm
1¼ × 4	1 × 3½	25 × 89 mm	2 × 12	1½ × 11¼	38 × 286 mm
1¼ × 6	1 × 5½	25 × 140 mm	3 × 6	2½ × 5½	64 × 140 mm
1¼ × 8	1 × 7¼	25 × 184 mm	4 × 4	3½ × 3½	89 × 89 mm
1¼ × 10	1 × 9¼	25 × 235 mm	4 × 6	3½ × 5½	89 × 140 mm
1¼ × 12	1 × 11¼	25 × 286 mm			

Metric Conversions

To Convert:	To:	Multiply by:	To Convert:	To:	Multiply by:
Inches	Millimeters	25.4	Millimeters	Inches	0.039
Inches	Centimeters	2.54	Centimeters	Inches	0.394
Feet	Meters	0.305	Meters	Feet	3.28
Yards	Meters	0.914	Meters	Yards	1.09
Square inches	Square centimeters	6.45	Square centimeters	Square inches	0.155
Square feet	Square meters	0.093	Square meters	Square feet	10.8
Square yards	Square meters	0.836	Square meters	Square yards	1.2
Ounces	Milliliters	30.0	Milliliters	Ounces	.033
Pints (U.S.)	Liters	0.473 (Imp. 0.568)	Liters	Pints (U.S.)	2.114 (Imp. 1.76)
Quarts (U.S.)	Liters	0.946 (Imp. 1.136)	Liters	Quarts (U.S.)	1.057 (Imp. 0.88)
Gallons (U.S.)	Liters	3.785 (Imp. 4.546)	Liters	Gallons (U.S.)	0.264 (Imp. 0.22)
Ounces	Grams	28.4	Grams	Ounces	0.035
Pounds	Kilograms	0.454	Kilograms	Pounds	2.2

Counterbore, Shank & Pilot Hole Diameters

Screw Size	Counterbore Diameter for Screw Head (in inches)	Clearance Hole for Screw Shank (in inches)	Pilot Hole Diameter	
			Hard Wood (in inches)	Soft Wood (in inches)
#1	.146 (⁹⁄₆₄)	⁵⁄₆₄	³⁄₆₄	¹⁄₃₂
#2	¼	³⁄₃₂	³⁄₆₄	¹⁄₃₂
#3	¼	⁷⁄₆₄	¹⁄₁₆	³⁄₆₄
#4	¼	⅛	¹⁄₁₆	³⁄₆₄
#5	¼	⅛	⁵⁄₆₄	¹⁄₁₆
#6	⁵⁄₁₆	⁹⁄₆₄	³⁄₃₂	⁵⁄₆₄
#7	⁵⁄₁₆	⁵⁄₃₂	³⁄₃₂	⁵⁄₆₄
#8	⅜	¹¹⁄₆₄	⅛	³⁄₃₂
#9	⅜	¹¹⁄₆₄	⅛	³⁄₃₂
#10	⅜	³⁄₁₆	⅛	⁷⁄₆₄
#11	½	³⁄₁₆	⁵⁄₃₂	⁹⁄₆₄
#12	½	⁷⁄₃₂	⁹⁄₆₄	⅛

Index

A

Acrylic carpet, about, 22
Adhesive
    described, 11
    for wood floor planks, 94
Alcoholic beverages, removing
    from carpet, 265
    from ceramic tile floors, 263
    from laminate floors, 264
    from resilient floors, 264
Anti-squeak hardware, installing, 238
Appliances, 13, 51
Asbestos in flooring, 11, 252
Attic floors
    about, 76
    building with new joists, 78–79
    reinforcing, 63
    strengthening, 76
    subflooring, installing, 79

B

Baby thresholds, described, 91
Bamboo floors
    about, 16, 102
    ideas, 35, 41, 44, 103
    strip, installing step-by-step, 104–107
    temperature/humidity range for, 102
Baseboards
    described, 91
    installing, 241
    protecting when painting, 219
    removing, 52
Basement floors
    about, 72
    concrete floor leveler, applying, 73
    concrete, patching, 73
    subfloor, building, 74–75
    vapor barrier, 63
    See also Concrete entries
Beater blocks, making & using, 237
Blind-nailing, described, 246
Blood, removing
    from carpet, 265
    from ceramic tile floors, 263
Bonded rubber roll flooring, installing
    about, 168
    step-by-step, 169–171
Bonded wood strip floor, installing, 98–99
Bronze, removing from concrete floors, 263
Buckled floorboards, fixing, 239
Bulging joists, repairing, 60
Bullnose base trim, installing, 151
Burn marks, removing from carpet, 265
Burns
    in carpet, repairing, 256
    in resilient flooring, repairing, 252–255
Butter, removing from carpet, 265

C

Candle wax, removing from carpet, 265
Candy, removing from carpet, 265

Carpet
    about, 22–23, 184
    burns & stains, repairing, 256
    buying, 184
    existing, evaluating, 12
    ideas, 29, 31, 32, 36, 40
    loose, restretching, 257
    loose seams, gluing, 257
    maintenance tips, 265
    removing, 55
    spot damage, repairing, 256, 265
    types of, 23
Carpet, installing
    around partition walls, 201
    cutouts, making, 205
    cutting & seaming, 196–201
    padding, 195
    planning & layout, 186–187
    on stairs, 187, 206–207
    stretching & securing, 202–205
    tackless strips, 194
    tools & materials, 188–191
    transitions, about, 192
    transitions, with metal carpet bars, 193
    transitions, with tackless strips, 193
Carpet reducers, described, 91
Carpet squares, installing
    about, 208
    step-by-step, 209–211
Cementboard underlayment
    for ceramic tile floors, 140
    installing, 66–67
Ceramic tile floors
    about, 20
    bullnose base trim, installing, 151
    cutting, 142–143
    existing, evaluating, 12, 13
    ideas, 29, 31, 33, 43
    installing overview, 144
    installing step-by-step, 145–150
    maintenance tips, 263
    materials for installing, 141
    removing, 54
    tools for installing, 141
    underlayment for, 140
Chewing gum, removing from carpet, 265
Chocolate, removing from carpet, 265
Club soda for carpet stains, 265
Coffee, removing from ceramic tile floors, 263
Combination tiles
    about, 156–157
    installing, 158–159
Concrete base, underlayment panels
    installation and, 70–71
Concrete floors
    ideas, 32, 39
    leveler, applying, 73
    maintenance tips, 262, 263
    patching, 73

Concrete floors, finishing
    about, 222
    cleaning & etching step-by-step, 224–225
    painting, 227
    sealing, 226
    tools & materials, 223
Copper, removing from concrete floors, 263
Cork flooring ideas, 44, 132
Cork soundproofing underlayment, installing, 68–69
Cork tiles, installing
    about, 132
    ideas, 132
    step-by-step, 133–135
Counterbores, plugging, 95
Cove moldings, vinyl, 183
Cracked joists, repairing, 61
Crayon, removing
    from carpet, 265
    from laminate floors, 264
    from resilient floors, 264
Cumaru wood, 15

D

Damaged floorboards, replacing, 244–247
Dark stains, removing
    from concrete floors, 263
    from wood floors, 262
Denatured alcohol, using, 242
Design, 24–25
Door casings, sliding tiles under, 125
Drum sanders, sandpapers for, 231
Dry-backed resilient tiles, installing step-by-step, 128–130

E

Eco-friendly linoleum, 19
Eco-friendly wood, 16
Edgers, sandpapers for, 231
Eggs, removing from carpet, 265
Electrical service for underfloor radiant heat systems, 80, 81, 82
Engineered wood flooring
    about, 17
    idea, 89
Excrement, removing from carpet, 265

F

Facenailing, 246
Floating laminate flooring
    about, 17, 112
    cutting, 117
    idea, 113
    installing step-by-step, 114–116
    marking for cutting, 117
    measuring for, 112
    thresholds & moldings, 91
Floor anatomy, 11

Floorboards
    damaged, replacing, 244–247
    loose or buckled, fixing, 239
Floor covering removal
    basics, 50
    carpet, 55
    ceramic tile, 54
    resilient tile, 54
    sheet vinyl flooring, 53
    tools for, 48–49
Floor leveler, 59
Floors, evaluating existing, 12–13
Food stains, removing
    from carpet, 265
    from ceramic tile floors, 263
    from laminate floors, 264
    from resilient floors, 264
    from wood floors, 262
Fruit juice, removing
    from carpet, 265
    from ceramic tile floors, 263
    from laminate floors, 264
    from resilient floors, 264
FSC-Certified wood, 16
Full-spread sheet vinyl, installing, 182
Fully bonded wood strip floor, installing, 98–99
Furniture polish, removing from carpet, 265

G
Glass tiles
    about, 21, 154
    bullnose base trim, installing, 151
    cutting, 142–143
    ideas, 30, 38, 45, 154, 155
    installing overview, 144
    installing step-by-step, 145–150
    materials for installing, 141
    tools for installing, 141
    underlayment for, 140
Granite tiles, 20, 21
Gravy, removing from carpet, 265
Grease, removing
    from carpet, 265
    from ceramic tile floors, 263
    from concrete floors, 263
    from wood floors, 262
Grooves in hardwood floors, trimming, 246

H
Hardwood floors
    about, 14, 88
    bonded wood strips, installing, 98–99
    cutting, 92
    eco-friendly, 16
    existing, evaluating, 12, 13
    exotic, 15
    ideas, 26, 27, 28, 30, 33, 34, 37, 38, 43
    plank, installing step-by-step, 93–97
    thresholds & moldings, 91
    tools, 90
Heat systems, installing underfloor radiant
    components, 80
    step-by-step, 82–85
    tips, 81

Heel marks, removing
    from laminate floors, 264
    from resilient floors, 264
Holes, patching in wood floors, 243

I
Ink stains, removing
    from concrete floors, 263
    from laminate floors, 264
    from resilient floors, 264
    from wood floors, 262
Interlocking utility tiles, installing
    about, 164
    step-by-step, 165–167
Ipé wood, 15
Iron, removing from concrete floors, 263
Isolation membranes, 140

J
Joists
    attic floor, about, 76
    attic floor, adding sister, 77
    attic floor, building with new, 78–79
    described, 11
    repairing, 60–61
    squeaky floors and, 236
Juice, removing
    from carpet, 265
    from ceramic tile floors, 263
    from laminate floors, 264
    from resilient floors, 264

K
Ketchup, removing from carpet, 265
Knee kickers, using, 190

L
Lacquer, removing, 242
Laminate flooring
    about, 17, 112
    cross-section of plank, 248
    cutting, 117
    idea, 113
    installing step-by-step, 114–116
    maintenance tips, 264
    marking for cutting, 117
    measuring for, 112
    planks, replacing, 248–251
    thresholds & moldings, 91
Latex paint for colorwashing, 214
Latex paint, removing
    from ceramic tile floors, 263
    from concrete floors, 263
Leather tile idea, 43
Limestone tiles, 20–21
Linoleum, repairing, 252
Linoleum strips, installing, 124–125
Linoleum tiles, installing
    about, 19, 122
    ideas, 42, 122, 123
    step-by-step, 124–125
Linseed oil, finishing plank flooring with, 97
Lipstick, removing from laminate floors, 264
Loop-pile carpet, 23
Loose floorboards, fixing, 239

M
Marble tile floor idea, 39
Margarine, removing from carpet, 265
Marmoleum, about, 19
Materials, estimating amount needed, 10, 49
Medallions
    ideas, 26, 100
    installing, 100–101
Mildew, removing
    from ceramic tile floors, 263
    from concrete floors, 263
    from wood floors, 262
Moisture
    concrete floors and, 72, 224
    tile and, 258
Moldings
    baseboards, installing, 241
    components, 240
    damaged, removing, 240
    types, 91
    vinyl cove, 183
Mold, removing
    from ceramic tile floors, 263
    from concrete floors, 263
    from wood floors, 262
Mosaic tiles
    ideas, 41, 45
    installing step-by-step, 152–153
Motor oil, removing from carpet, 265
Mustard, removing
    from carpet, 265
    from ceramic tile floors, 263
    from resilient floors, 264

N
Nail polish, removing
    from carpet, 265
    from laminate floors, 264
    from resilient floors, 264
No-glue sheet vinyl, installing, 180–181
Nylon carpet, about, 22

O
Oak flooring, 14
Oil-based paint, removing
    from ceramic tile floors, 263
    from concrete floors, 263
Oil, finishing plank flooring with, 97
Oil, removing
    from carpet, 265
    from concrete floors, 263
    from wood floors, 262
Overlap reducers, described, 91

P
Painting
    concrete floors, 222–227
    tools, 219, 223
Paint, removing
    from ceramic tile floors, 263
    from concrete floors, 263
    from laminate floors, 264
    from resilient floors, 264
Palm flooring idea, 45

Parquet tiles
    about, 14, 88
    ideas, 34, 108
    installing on diagonal, 111
    installing step-by-step, 109–111
Patagonian Rosewood, 15
Penetrant finish for wood, 229
Perfume, removing from carpet, 265
Perimeter-bond sheet vinyl, installing, 178–179
Permanent marker, removing from resilient floors, 264
Pet stains, removing from wood floors, 262
Plank flooring
    about, 14
    bamboo strip, installing step-by-step, 104–107
    finishing unfinished, 97
    installing step-by-step installation, 93–97
    laminate planks, replacing, 248–251
    sections, replacing, 245–247
    width of floorboards, 88
Plank flooring, installing vinyl
    about, 118
    step-by-step, 120–121
    tips, 119
Planning
    checklist, 10
    design, 24–25
    measuring room, 49
    tools needed, 48–49
Plugs for counterbores, 95
Plush carpet, 23
Plywood underlayment
    for ceramic tile floors, 140
    installing, 65
Polyester carpet, about, 22
Polypropylene carpet, about, 22
Polyurethane floors
    dark stains, removing, 262
    minor scratches, fixing, 262
Polyurethane sealers
    about, 219
    applying, 233
Porcelain snap-lock tiles
    about, 160
    installing, 161–163
    replacing damaged, 163
Power miter saws, 48
Power stretchers, using, 190, 191
Preparation
    existing floor covering removal, 50, 53–55
    joist repair, 60–61
    subfloor repair, 58–59
    underlayment removal, 56–57
Primers, 219

Q
Quarry tile flooring idea, 41
Quarter rounds, described, 91

R
Radiant heat systems, installing underfloor

components, 80
step-by-step, 82–85
tips, 81
Reclaimed wood flooring, 16
Recycled rubber tiles, installing
    about, 136
    step-by-step, 137–139
Reducer strips, described, 91
Resilient flooring
    about, 18
    asbestos in pre-1980, 11
    existing, evaluating, 12, 13
    ideas, 28, 30
    maintenance tips, 264
    tools for installing, 175
    types, 18–19, 175
Resilient flooring, repairing
    about, 252
    sheet vinyl, patching, 253–254
    tiles, patching, 255
Resilient sheet vinyl, installing
    about, 174
    cutting templates, making, 177
    full-spread, 182
    no-glue, 180–181
    perimeter-bond, step-by-step, 178–179
    tips, 176
    tools, 175
    vinyl cove molding, 183
Resilient tiles
    about, 18
    idea, 43
    removing, 54
    replacing, 255
Resilient tiles, installing
    about, 126
    dry-backed, step-by-step, 128–130
    reference lines, making, 127
    self-adhesive, step-by-step, 131
Rooms, measuring, 49
Rosewood, 15
Rubber roll flooring, installing
    bonded, 168–171
    seamed, 172–173
Rugs, ideas for using, 27, 31, 38
Rust, removing
    from ceramic tile floors, 263
    from concrete floors, 263
    from resilient floors, 264

S
Safety
    equipment, 230
    ventilation, 51
    when working with tiles, 258
Sagging joists, repairing, 61
Salad dressing, removing from carpet, 265
Sandpapers for drum sanders & edgers, 231
Sandstone tiles, 20–21
Saxony-cut pile carpet, 23
Scratches
    minor in wood floors, fixing, 262
    in wood floors, patching, 243

Sealers
    for concrete floors, applying, 226
    for wood, 229
Seamed rubber roll flooring, installing, 172–173
Self-adhesive resilient tiles, installing step-by-step, 131
Sheet vinyl flooring
    about, 18–19
    removing, 53
    repairing, 252–254
Sheet vinyl flooring, installing
    about, 174
    cutting templates, making, 177
    full-spread, 182
    no-glue, 180–181
    perimeter-bond, step-by-step, 178–179
    tips, 176
    tools, 175
    vinyl cove molding, 183
Shellac, removing, 242
Shoe polish, removing
    from carpet, 265
    from laminate floors, 264
    from resilient floors, 264
Sister joists, adding for attic floors, 77
Slate tiles, 21
Snap-lock tiles, porcelain
    about, 160
    installing, 161–163
    replacing damaged, 163
Soft drinks, removing from carpet, 265
Solvents, using, 242
Soundproofing with cork underlayment, 68–69
Squeaky floors, fixing
    about, 236
    beater blocks and, 237
    loose floorboards, fastening, 239
Squeaky floors, preventing, 237, 238
Stains for wood
    described, 229
    removing, 243
Stains in carpet, repairing, 256
Stair nosing, described, 91
Stairs, carpeting, 187, 206–207
Stone tiles
    about, 20–21
    bullnose base trim, installing, 151
    cutting, 142–143
    installing overview, 144
    installing step-by-step, 145–150
    materials for installing, 141
    tools for installing, 141
    underlayment for, 140
Strip wood flooring
    about, 14
    bamboo strip, installing step-by-step, 104–107
    finishing unfinished, 97
    laminate planks, replacing, 248–251
    replacing sections, 245–247
    step-by-step installation, 93–97
    width of floorboards, 88
Subfloors
    attic, installing, 79

basement, building, 74–75
basement, wood for, 72
described, 11
existing, evaluating, 12
repairing, 58–59
squeaky floors and, 236
Surface finish for wood, 229
Synthetic carpet, 22
Syrup, removing from carpet, 265

T
Tar, removing
    from carpet, 265
    from laminate floors, 264
Tears in resilient flooring, repairing, 252–255
Terrazzo flooring, 21
Textured concrete flooring idea, 32
Thresholds, types of, 91
Tigerwood, 15
Tiles
    combination, installing, 156–159
    door casings, sliding under, 125
    ideas, 27, 34, 35, 36, 37, 40, 43
    interlocking utility, installing, 164–167
    outside corners, marking for, 130
    porcelain snap-lock, installing, 160–163
    regrouting, 259
    replacing, 260–261
    See also specific types of tiles
T-moldings, described, 91
Tongues & grooves, trimming, 246
Tools
    carpet installation, 188–191
    ceramic, glass & stone tile installation,
        141
    concrete floor finishing, 223
    floor covering removal, 48–49
    hardwood floor installation, 90
    painting, 219
    resilient sheet vinyl installation, 175
    wood floors refinishing, 229
Travertine tiles, 21
Trim moldings
    baseboards, installing, 241
    components, 240
    damaged, removing, 240
    types, 91
    vinyl cove, 183
Tungseed oil, finishing plank flooring
    with, 97

U
Underfloor radiant heat systems,
    installing
    components, 80
    step-by-step, 82–85
    tips, 81
Underlayment
    cementboard, installing, 66–67
    cork soundproofing, installing, 68–69
    described, 11, 64
    existing, evaluating, 12
    for hard tile floors, 140
    importance of, 63
    panels on concrete base, installing,
        70–71

plywood, installing, 65
    removing, 56–57
    tile replacement and, 258
    types, 64
Urine, removing from carpet, 265
Utility tiles, installing interlocking
    about, 164
    step-by-step, 165–167

V
Varnish, removing, 242
Vegetable oil, removing from carpet, 265
Velvet-cut pile carpet, 23
Ventilation, 51
Vinyl cove moldings, 183
Vinyl flooring
    about, 18–19
    See also Resilient vinyl flooring
        entries; Sheet vinyl flooring entries
Vinyl plank flooring, installing
    about, 118
    step-by-step, 120–121
    tips, 119
Vinyl tiles
    asbestos and, 252
    replacing, 255

W
Wax
    advantages of using, 229
    plank flooring, finishing with, 97
Waxed floors
    dark stains, removing, 262
    minor scratches, fixing, 262
    mold or mildew, removing, 262
    oil or grease, removing, 262
    surface damage, repairing, 262
Wax, removing
    from carpet, 265
    from hardwood floors, 242
    from laminate floors, 264
    from resilient floors, 264
Wenge wood, 15
Wine, removing
    from carpet, 265
    from ceramic tile floors, 263
    from laminate floors, 264
    from resilient floors, 264
Wood floor finishes
    about, 14
    aged & distressed, about, 214
    aged & distressed, applying, 217
    colorwashes, about, 214
    colorwashes, applying, 216
    colorwashes, options, 217
    colorwashes, variations, 215
    paint, about, 218
    paint, applying, 219–220
    paint, applying checkerboard pattern,
        221
    for plank flooring, 97
    stains, about, 214
    stains, applying to bare floors, 216
    stains, variations, 215
    types, 229

Wood floors
    about, 14, 88, 213
    bonded hardwood strips, installing,
        98–99
    eco-friendly, 16
    engineered, 17
    existing, evaluating, 12, 13
    exotic, 15
    hardwood, cutting, 92
    ideas, 26, 27, 28, 30, 33, 34, 37, 38, 43
    laminate, 17
    maintaining, 262
    plank, step-by-step installation, 93–97
    thresholds & moldings, 91
    tools, 90
    See also Bamboo floors
Wood floors, refinishing
    about, 228
    preparation, 230
    step-by-step, 231–233
    tools & materials, 229
    types of finishes, 229
Wood floors, repairing
    about, 242
    cleaning & renewing, 242
    damaged floorboards, replacing,
        244–247
    holes, patching, 243
    laminate planks, 248–251
    scratches, patching, 243
    squeaky, fixing, 236–237
    squeaky, fixing loose floorboards, 239
    squeaky, installing anti-squeak
    hardware, 238
    stains, removing, 243
    tongues & grooves, trimming, 246
Wool carpet, 22